MW00323999

"Every day is another opportunity to make our mark on the world, and Katie DePaola is certainly making her mark. *At Least You Look Good* is a battle cry to 'glow through what you go through' and a must-read for anyone pursuing their purpose in the midst of life's surprises."

—**Denise Lee**, founder and CEO of Alala

"We must always stand up for what we believe in and what we value. This starts with believing in and standing up for ourselves in the face of adversity. Katie's courage in sharing her story provides a dose of hope, which we need now more than ever. Keep glowing. You are beautiful and worthy of everything you dream of."

—**Amy Lefévre**, model and entrepreneur

"Katie's humor and realistic outlook are refreshing and inspiring. *At Least You Look Good* teaches the reader to embrace love and loss, light and shadow. Katie's story is an example of the power of reflecting on your past in order to heal and progress towards the future destined for you."

—**vp wright**, social entrepreneur and founder of The Creative's Corner™

"*At Least You Look Good* hits the nail on the head with the challenges women experience around beauty. A profound and refreshing approach to love, loss and discovering your true self."

—**Nikoletta Skarlatos**, award-winning Hollywood makeup artist and wellness spokesperson

"Katie wrote a book straight out of her heart space. Her raw account weaved in with her masterful writing style shows us how healing is done... and lets us know we can do the same. [She has] made healing fascinating and real. All of us can move from pain to healing with Katie's inspiration."

—**Debra Silverman**, astrologer and author of *The Missing Element*

"Strong women continue to raise the bar and Katie DePaola is one of them. Life will continue to challenge us, but as women, it's our job to be bold and become a force for good. Katie's honesty, as she learns to not only survive but thrive, is just what the world needs to get inspired and stay there."

—**Stefania Okolie**, designer and founder of Solely Fit

"We all have a story to tell. Having the confidence to show up and share that story is what makes all the difference. When we are willing to face our stories head-on, we can find purpose and possibility on the other side. Katie's approach to manifesting your desires and finding purpose in pain are exactly what's needed in these challenging times."

—**Debra Alfarone**, Emmy Award-winning TV journalist

"Just because you've been through hard things doesn't mean you can't create a brand. In fact, your brand and your story can be exactly what gets people to connect with you in an authentic way. Watching Katie and her business evolve has been nothing short of inspiring. Cue the confetti! You really can glow through whatever you go through."

—**Caroline Kalentzos**, Boss Doll® and CEO of POSH PR® and The Caroline Doll

At Least You Look Good

LEARNING TO
GLOW THROUGH
WHAT YOU GO
THROUGH

KATIE DEPAOLA

ISBN: 978-1-951407-37-1 Hardcover

ISBN: 978-1-951407-35-3 Paperback

ISBN: 978-1-951407-36-0 eBook

DISCLAIMER

This work is non-fiction and, as such, reflects the author's memory of the experiences. Many of the names and identifying characteristics of the individuals featured in this book have been changed to protect their privacy and certain individuals are composites. Dialogue and events have been recreated; in some cases, conversations were edited to convey their substance rather than written exactly as they occurred.

To all the girls who have walked through fire to become the women they are today.

And, of course, my brother Bo.

CONTENTS

INTRODUCTION

"Nothing is absolute. Everything changes, everything moves, everything revolves, everything flies and goes away."
—Frida Kahlo

I've always been a hopeless romantic. It didn't matter how many heartbreaks I went through or how much pain I endured. I believed that eventually, the right love would come, and when it did, it would last forever. As a kid, forever seemed like a long time. It seemed like, well, forever. But forever didn't seem like just a timeline to me. Forever seemed like an approach, a way of loving that was eternal, lasting and essentially perfect. Forever love would be without pain. I believed that if I could just find the perfect love, then the perfect life would come with it. Then, finally, everything would feel okay.

It wasn't that things weren't okay, though. In fact, everything was okay, and that was precisely the problem. I wanted more. I was unimpressed with life. I was disappointed by the dullness and the monotony of the day to day. By the start of 2015, to the outside world, it looked like I was doing pretty well. I had just started my third company, Inner Glow Circle, and bought my second condo in Washington, D.C. I had a wildly supportive family, lots of great friends, a few pairs of designer shoes and all the Whole Foods I could ask for.

But something felt wrong, really wrong, and it took years of healing to understand that although there wasn't anything wrong with me, there was a lot wrong with the world. I was a highly sensitive person living in an increasingly toxic world. The toxicity wasn't limited to my food or my beauty products. It had also seeped into my mind. I had been fed decades of defunct messaging about love, happiness, success and what it meant to be a woman.

I was tired of being judged by how I looked, how cute my apartment was or how happy my family looked on our Christmas card. The other catch-22, though, was that I liked looking good. When I looked good, I felt less pain.

By the end of 2015, I felt completely alone. I was exhausted by all the dead ends, the failed attempts, the trying and trying and trying. I didn't look sick. I didn't look like I was grieving. I didn't look like I'd just escaped an abusive relationship. But I had, and that's what was confusing. Everyone said I looked good, but I felt like shit.

I knew I had to be nearing the end of a cycle. I believed in God and there was no way She wanted me to suffer forever. I was meant for that forever love.

Surely, the pain was meant to teach me something, but what?

My name is Katie DePaola and I'm a mindset and resilience expert. I help people find healing, meaning and growth after—and often while—they go through the biggest challenges of their lives.

I'm assuming if you're reading this that you've been through some shit. You've had your heart torn out. You've lost someone you love. You've been overlooked, underpaid, taken advantage of or completely misled. You've been told you're not worthy, that your dreams are too big, that you should "keep your day job" and that you should just be grateful for what you have.

The problem is that you're not content. You want more.

There's a careful balance between fighting for opportunity and letting it come to you. The answer, for me, was to let up on some of the fight and start allowing myself to surrender. To walk the line between surviving and thriving. It wasn't a single-lane approach.

I didn't only have to go through difficult moments. I could glow through them as they were happening. My personal mantra became, "Glow through what you go through." This is still my mantra today. It's also part of the mission of my company, Inner Glow Circle, which helps women find their purpose and get paid to live it.

This book is less about self-help and more about self-awareness. It's about self-advocacy, finding your voice and trusting yourself along the way. It's about managing the ups and downs of love and loss, and figuring out how to find the glow in the dark without being sucked into the world of toxic positivity.

Glowing through what I go through is my number one strategy for moving forward, making peace with life and creating beauty from pain.

Can you glow through what you go through? What path can you take to get there?

These are the questions of this book.

The human brain is hardwired toward negativity. The road most traveled is one of pessimism, limited possibility and feeling like a victim. But who wants to be on that road forever?

Learning to glow through what you go through is ultimately mindset work. In pivotal moments, many times a day, you must take the thought less traveled. It's work. But I promise it's worth it.

I now live my life by a handful of rules. They've helped me get through losing my brother, beat Lyme disease after a 10-year battle and recover from the most terrifying relationship I could have ever imagined.

Most importantly, these rules have allowed me to keep evolving my life, my business and myself along the way. I took Inner Glow Circle from a self-funded startup to a million-dollar business, trained hundreds of life coaches, built a loyal team, created a solid business partnership, attracted the best friends I've ever had and opened my heart to love again and again. I've become the woman I've always wanted to be—well, almost.

Here are my top five rules of life:

1. Life gets to get better and better.
2. Take giving up off the table.
3. Ask what's possible, not what's probable.
4. It's *this* or something better, always.
5. What's meant for me can't miss me.

When I lost my brother, he was gone but he was everywhere. When I had Lyme, I lost my health, but I found my purpose. When my relationship ended, I lost who I thought I was, but discovered who I wanted to become.

For most of my life, I was your typical people pleaser.

It's not that I don't listen to other people's opinions anymore. It's just that I care about my opinion of me the most. When it comes to everyone else, I've decided my purpose is to challenge the norm and push others to do the same.

I want this book to encourage that boldness within you. I want my stories to inspire you to own your desires, stop apologizing for wanting more, fall in and out of love a million times and finally go for your dreams.

PART ONE
BASICS

ONE

CHOOSING MIRACLES

"Life isn't about waiting for the storm to pass. It's about learning how to dance in the rain."
—Vivian Greene

I was sitting in the car in my parents' driveway when I opened the email. It would be nine more months before I could see a doctor who could help me.

The problem was, I didn't have nine months. My body was tired and my heart was split in two. My brother was never coming back, and I'd been, unknowingly, living with Lyme disease for a decade now.

I broke down. Tears poured out of my eyes and snot ran down my face. There, alone in the car, I started speaking out loud.

"What is going on? Why am I still struggling so badly? And why have I been allowing myself to live like this? What part of me is accepting this level of pain, grief and sadness year after year?"

The answer I heard back changed everything.

"You haven't decided," I heard from somewhere. Maybe it was God, maybe it was a future version of myself.

"What?" I asked back.

"You haven't decided," I heard again.

All of a sudden, like in a movie, I saw my future flash before my eyes. I saw myself speaking, teaching, traveling, getting married, becoming a mom and appearing on TV. I saw all the things I'd wanted since I was a kid.

I knew a lot of these future visions wouldn't be possible if I wasn't mentally, emotionally and physically well. I also knew a part of me had accepted staying sick for a long time. The voice was right. I hadn't decided I was staying here. I was one foot in and one foot out in my own life. But I needed to decide, and soon, because I was running out of time.

"I'm not done with this life," I said out loud. "In fact, I'm just getting started. I'm going to keep building my company, finish my book, have a beautiful family and travel the world. I'm going to make the impact I came here to make."

I decided at that moment that I didn't have to die along with my brother. I would live because he couldn't.

Once I made that decision, the miracles started to pour in. Once I took giving up off the table, everything changed.

It didn't matter what challenges life would bring me. From here on out, I would glow through what I go through.

TWO

FEAR OF GLOWING

"I stand in the mist and cry, thinking of myself standing in the mist and crying, and wondering if I will ever be able to use this experience in a book."

—Erica Jong

My earliest childhood journals are evidence of my original plan for myself. All I knew was that I wanted to be famous and to help people. I didn't know what I wanted to be famous *for* or *how* I wanted to help people. I just envisioned a big, expansive life where people knew who I was and respected whatever I created. As I got older, I dreamt of using clothes, makeup, lingerie, healthy foods, the internet and TV to make a positive impact on women across the world. I never dreamed I would end up creating courses, speaking, teaching and building a real company. I thought companies were run by men.

In middle school, my friend and I started what was technically my first business. A branding expert from a young age, I wrote the company tagline: *Live so that you glow*. We printed business cards in my parents' basement and created our first product, glass bowls with handwritten inspirational quotes. Neither the business cards nor the bowls ever made it out of the basement, but they were proof that I could bring a vision to reality.

In high school, I started making early plans for the company I run today. In my journal, I wrote about my idea to create an online platform where younger girls could ask older girls their most pressing questions and get honest answers. I was interested in coaching and mentoring long before I knew what coaching and mentoring were.

In college, I joined a sorority and got involved with its new member recruitment efforts. Some people said that joining a sorority was like paying for your friends, but I saw depth and potential. Annual dues were substantial, but I recognized a huge business opportunity in connecting like-minded women. I wanted to learn everything I could.

After college, I moved to New York City, hoping to find my true path in life. I joined the board of a nonprofit and it was through that experience that I got the opportunity to meet Gabrielle Bernstein for the first time. I went to a talk she was giving at an Equinox fitness club on the Upper East Side.

I was speechless as I listened to Gabby talk about her goal to become the happiest person she knew. I had an out-of-body experience as I watched her. It felt like I was seeing a vision of my own future. Gabby was spiritual, successful and cool. More importantly, her career was centered around helping people. After the presentation, I bought Gabby's book and tore through it.

Gabby was just starting her career in the self-help industry and my encounter with her was a turning point in my quest to live a purpose-driven life. It was the moment I realized that starting a company could be about more than just printing business cards, making a business plan and recruiting potential customers. I could create a business based on a mission and design a brand around ideas that inspired me and impacted others.

Six months later, I went to a writing retreat, where I met Erica Jong, the feminist author of *Fear of Flying*. Erica spoke with incredible power as she encouraged us to write the story our soul needed us to tell. After I read to the group what I'd written, Erica looked me square in the eye. "You have a book in you." That was all I needed to activate my belief in myself. "Write something that unlocks who you are," she said. "Be yourself, discover yourself and write in your own voice."

How was I supposed to know what my own voice sounded like? I'd never used it.

My calling was to *create* something, but what? And, with all the crazy things going on in my personal life, how?

The truth was that there had been crazy things going on in my personal life for a long time—and despite them, I continued to work toward my purpose. My purpose—specifically, my work as a mindset and resilience expert and the founder of Inner Glow Circle—became my glow in the dark. I tell people that I built my business from the bed, the bathtub and over 30 doctors' offices because I did. In the end, my business saved me. Even on the hardest days, I had something to show up for.

I didn't *create* the hard things that happened in my life, but they were there, so I had to decide what I was going to do with them. I started to ask myself if I could take my biggest challenges and turn them into my greatest opportunities.

THREE
THE LIE OF LOOKING GOOD

"It's not the load that breaks you down, it's the way you carry it."
—Lena Horne

Some people think life is easier when you look a certain way, but the reality is that when you're pretty on the outside, people often don't believe anything could be wrong on the inside. They assume your problems are privileged and superficial, even if they're *really* real. I know from experience. Too many times, I've been the girl focused on looking good on the outside while deeply struggling on the inside. Too many times, how I look has been the only thing I could control. And too many times, people around me have assumed the way I looked on the outside meant whatever I was dealing with on the inside couldn't be *that bad*.

Not long ago, I found myself at my psychiatrist's office during one of the worst weeks I'd had in a long time. I'd been feeling down for months, and the medication trials she was running on me were making my mental health worse instead of better. Paxil was giving me painfully dry eyes, while Prozac had me hiccupping through my entire hot yoga class. I was a total mess, my mindset was in the gutter and although I didn't really need an expensive out-of-network doctor's appointment to confirm it, I was there anyway, eagerly searching for a solution.

I was wearing a white crop top and fire-engine red leggings that cinched my waist.

"How are you feeling?" my doctor asked excitedly. Usually, I liked that she was happy and upbeat. On this particular day, her peppy attitude was annoying.

"Really, really bad," I said.

"Well, at least you look good," she responded, smiling.

I stared at her blankly. Of course I looked good. I had just gotten a spray tan and a blowout. But the whole reason I was working with a psychiatrist was so that she could see past all the layers of protection I had created for myself.

———

THE ACT of sizing each other up based on outward appearances isn't just a middle school phenomenon reserved for cafeteria conversations about who's hot and who's not. It's an attempt at social survival. The brain makes judgment calls all day based on outward appearances and I'm far from innocent. Even though I hate feeling seen as the pretty girl with no real problems, I can still be incredibly judgmental myself. But beauty on the outside is not reflective of what's happening on the inside.

It's a mistake to hyper-focus on appearances and ignore the emotional complexities that come with being human, but I wasn't born or raised with this awareness. In my family, looking good wasn't just the norm. It was the expectation. Things *had* to look good. Generally, they did. The first time my high school boyfriend came to my family Christmas, his only comment was that everyone was good-looking. I was confused. Weren't people *supposed* to look good?

We all get the advice in childhood not to judge a book by its cover and yet it's very hard advice to follow. I understand my privilege. I'm white. I'm educated. I'm healthy—at the moment. And with a little makeup, I'm objectively good-looking. Just because I *look* good doesn't mean I *feel* good though, and even when looking good *and* feeling good do align, you can't imagine the inner and outer work it's taken me to get there. Why do you think my American Express bill is so high?

The disconnect between looking good and feeling good is similar to the disconnect between feeling lit up by a big win and days later, feeling totally empty inside. You go from reaching a milestone and celebrating with friends to sitting alone in your office or bedroom, wondering what the hell you're doing with your life. Dopamine doesn't last forever. Thanks to my work as a coach, I know these ups and downs are part of the process of growth and transformation.

Life isn't linear. It's actually the opposite, and if your brain works anything like mine—obsessive-compulsive tendencies and all—it's difficult to wrap your head around that information. Obviously, we can't force life into the straight line we want it to be. But we can move forward despite the discomfort of not knowing how it's going to unfold.

FOUR

THE CYCLE OF LOVING AND LOSING

"Gratitude unlocks the fullness of life. It turns what we have into enough, and more. It turns denial into acceptance, chaos to order, confusion to clarity."
—Melody Beattie

Every time you lose something, you gain something else, because for everything gained, something equal is lost—and for everything lost, something equal is gained. It's the Law of Equal Exchange. If we let it flow and don't put up a fight, energy always replaces itself. Eventually, things balance out.

People talk a lot about failing forward as a key to success. I like to call it "loving losing." If you can learn how to lose with grace, gratitude and an eye toward the future, you'll find it easier to rise back up again. Figuring out how to lose with purpose and intention gives you a shot at loving bigger and better than ever before.

I've learned from experience that grief is the deepest form of gratitude. Grief is how we honor what we once had. It is how we pay our respects. But it doesn't always feel like that, especially in the beginning, when grief is a new and unfamiliar friend.

When I experienced loss, I asked myself how grief and gratitude fit together. I was intrigued by how it was possible to hold both feelings at once. I felt happy one moment and sad the next. My brain struggled to make sense of it. How could I simultaneously grieve my brother's death and be grateful for his life?

I started tracking my own grief. I realized within every small loss, there was also some small blessing. Sometimes, the blessing was obvious. Sometimes I had to dig for it. But in the end, there was always something to be grateful for.

Part of your purpose is to create the things you wish existed. I wished there was a map for grief, so I created one. I spent years studying the relationship between loving and losing—and mapping out how to get from one to the other so I could rise faster and show you how to do the same. To start, you must surrender your resistance, give up who you think you are and become open to integrating your glow and your dark.

Every time I lost something, I had to find the gift in it. When I say I *had to*, I mean that. It was *required* for my survival. I had to find a way to be grateful for all of it—the love *and* the loss.

It was a radical, radical thought and an unreasonable request, but it's how I changed the experience of my life. Everything difficult can also be a gift. Every challenge has a secret present. You just have to be willing to unwrap it.

The Cycle of Loving and Losing is the map for grief I

made to explain the process I used to survive my sadness and breathe new life into my world.

The Cycle of Loving and Losing

Let's start with making love. I understand the phrase commonly refers to the act of having sex, but here, I'm talking about creation itself, which requires the sacred, sensual energy of life. Making love is about making magic, even when you think all the magic has disappeared. It's about staying awake, opening and surrendering to life, even when you want to escape or shut down. Most of all, it's about belief and possibility. Making love will renew you when you fear that everything good has been taken away.

Love will always ask you to lose. When you love big, it's not just about you anymore.

Unconditional love rewrites the rules, breaks down barriers and inspires you to give regardless of what you receive in return.

In the process of losing, you will be forced to release your attachments and surrender what you thought was yours. It may be difficult but letting go is the most expansive choice you can make. Letting go is the key to the shift. It's where you admit you don't have all the answers and ask for divine guidance along the way. It's not a submission. It's an opening even further.

When you finally let go, you unlock the door to being free. In your freedom, love can find its way back to you. You end up making love all over again; now, a bit more aware of the beauty of loss, the inevitability of it all. You won't grip so tightly this time, but you will love bigger than ever before, because you won't be afraid of what's to come. You've already accepted the losing in loving—and the loving in losing.

It hurts to get hurt, but there's another way through suffering and pain. Loss can be a cycle that takes you right back to love.

The day will come when you will lose the things you love. But you'll have peace in knowing that nothing can ever leave you completely because love always comes back.

You just have to open the door and let it in.

If you shortcut The Cycle of Loving and Losing, the irony is this: Losing is exactly what makes space for loving again. Loving and losing are like breathing—the inhale is loving and the exhale is losing. Don't sit around preparing yourself to lose everything you love. Instead, prepare yourself to love more expansively each time.

All those people who swear off love after one heartbreak are cheating themselves of the miracle that exists in loving again. Loving again is bigger than loving the first time. You might think it's the other way around, that the first love is always the best love, but that's not true. Love grows as you do, as you allow it, as you make space for it.

When I experienced a lot of loss at once, my world fell apart. I felt like nothing because I realized I *was* nothing. But then something happened. As soon as I realized I was nothing, I also realized I was everything. No matter how much I lost, I could always come back to me.

I can't possibly understand exactly what you've experienced, the fires you've walked through or the love you've had to lose, but I do know that you've survived life's challenges to be here today. I also know there's another side, where the grief lessens and the hurt no longer keeps you up at night. I'm not asking you to step over your sadness, deny your emotions or rush through your pain. I'm inviting you to honor it so deeply that you understand its role as a teacher and integrate its lessons so you can love and live even larger.

My way won't work for everyone, but it will work for some. It won't be a complete solution, but it might take you a step further. It won't be your end, but it could be your new beginning.

The writing retreat with Erica Jong was one of *my* new beginnings, a pivotal moment that gave me my first real dose of confidence and a glimpse of myself as someone truly worthy of the ambitions I dreamed of since I was a little girl. The book you have in your hands is the story Erica knew 10 years ago I would have to tell. It's the story of what my life's greatest teachers—body, beauty and boys—have taught me about losing, letting go, being free and making love all over again.

Throughout this book, I'm going to be sharing with you some of the prayers I wrote in my journal. Here's the first one:

God, change me into the one
Who sees the opportunity in everything.
Let my joy be as deep as my grief,
And my laugh be as loud as my cry.
Let me feel the expansiveness

Of this human experience.
Make me into the one who trusts
Myself, my instincts and my intuition.
Teach me to feel again—
And to dance through my feelings.
Show me how to love losing,
So I can open my heart to love again.

PART TWO
BODY

FIVE

EXISTENTIAL ANXIETY

"I want to feel what I feel. Even if it's not happiness."

—Toni Morrison

I swear I was born anxious. I was born anxious about my purpose in life.

Existential anxiety happens when you have so much stress and angst over the meaning of life that it gets in the way of your day-to-day routine. You can spend days, weeks, months and even years questioning your existence. It's distracting, time-consuming and sounds something like this:

Why am I here?
What's the point of life?
What if I never fulfill my purpose?
What if everything I'm doing is just a waste of time?

People with existential anxiety wrestle with these ques-

tions on a near-constant basis. I'm no exception. I was basically born stressed out. Growing up, I would get stressed
about school, sports and friends, but more than that, I was
stressed about what I was doing here on Earth.

I was never the kid asking, "Are we there yet?" I
couldn't even get "there" mentally, because I was trying to
figure out why I was "here" in the first place.

Have you ever experienced existential anxiety? Take it
from an expert: There are many versions. You might find
yourself constantly wondering if you're *really* supposed to
be here on Earth or if someone—maybe God, maybe your
mom—made a giant mistake. You might feel uncomfortable
in your own body—just crunchy, achy and *weird*. You might
feel totally alone even in a big group. One minute, you're on
the inside, present and engaged in the conversation. The
next, you're on the outside and analyzing *everything*.

If you have existential anxiety, one word runs your
life: *why?*

Why am I at this party?
Why am I talking to this guy?
Why am I friends with these people?

Before you know it, you're right back to "*Wait, why* am *I
here, like,* at all?" You hope that when you zoom out and
look at the big picture, your deep internal questions will
start to make more sense, but they actually make everything
more complicated.

Based on my own experience, I can't say existential
anxiety causes depression, but it definitely causes analysis
paralysis, which gets exhausting. At a certain point, I was
tired of thinking about my own existence. I just wanted to

relax and live my best life. If this rings a bell for you, it's possible you've been dealing with existential anxiety too.

Existential anxiety can be triggered by a major trauma, such as a tragic death, a devastating breakup, a serious diagnosis, a job loss or the dissolution of anything else you were really counting on working out. Your life experiences give you purpose and direction, and when they don't turn out the way you imagined, you're often left with a stack of questions, a bucket of tears and nothing but a box of tissues to clean up the mess.

I wish I could say my existential anxiety started when I got sick, got worse when my brother died and went to the next level when my ex-fiancé committed himself to a psychiatric hospital, but the incessant questions began much earlier than all that. Not to get all Lady Gaga on you, but I'm pretty sure I was born this way. For as long as I can remember, I've been anxious about my purpose.

SIX

FROM ANXIETY TO ACTION

"We know only too well that what we are doing is nothing more than a drop in the ocean. But if the drop were not there, the ocean would be missing something."

—Mother Teresa

My generalized anxiety started when I was five years old. I remember lying on the floor in my kindergarten classroom, unable to fall asleep during nap time because I was worried about whether the boy I had a crush on also had a crush on me. Even then, my mind raced with unnecessary anxious thoughts.

The existential anxiety? I don't remember the exact origin, but I know the feelings started boiling over when I was 11 or 12. I'd read one too many stories from *Chicken Soup for the Teenage Soul* and didn't know what to do with all my feelings. Have you ever read those books? They're supposed to be inspiring, but they're *really* serious.

Chicken Soup told stories of kids getting terminally ill, losing their parents, experiencing severe bullying and self-harming. Most of it was downright depressing to read, especially since I was already a sensitive preteen. As an adult, I know I'm an empath, which puts my intense response to those books into perspective. Empaths feel other people's feelings. If I'm talking to someone who's sad, I can walk away from the conversation feeling sad, especially if I don't remember to protect my energy. Even when I was a tween, reading these depressing stories in *Chicken Soup* made me feel depressed.

To cope with the sadness I seemed to have "caught" from these stories, I started praying and journaling. I've heard people say prayer is talking to God and meditation is listening to God's answers. I learned how to pray from my parents, but I taught myself how to listen through my journal. I asked God how I could help kids like the ones I read about. I also asked what I was meant to be doing with my life. *I want to be famous,* I'd write over and over in my journal. I wasn't sure how to make the connection between helping people and fame or between fame and purpose, but I trusted my instincts and wrote what I felt.

Night after night, I was like a detective searching for the real meaning of life in those pages. I didn't share my late-night existential binges with anyone. No one else at school was talking about how cool it was to stay up until midnight trying to hack the nature of existence, so I figured it wasn't a thing other preteens were doing. My existential escapades were a secret kept between me and my journal.

As I got older, I couldn't imagine I was the only one curious about my existence. Now and then, casually, maybe even after a drink or two, I'd ask friends, "Why do you think we're here?"

"Here, like, at this party?" my high school friends would say.

"No, like, here in general."

"Here at Vanderbilt?" my college friends would ask.

"No!" I'd say. Then, I'd pause and reconsider. Did I really want to go down the existential rabbit hole in a frat house? "Wait, yes. Here at Vandy."

"My mom is an alum. You?"

"It's the best school I got into."

Subject changed. Fast.

I'm not much of a drinker, and not because I have a problem with alcohol. I'm not much of a drinker because no one wants to drink with me. This might not surprise you, but most people don't feel inspired to talk about deep philosophy after having a few.

I'd been uncomfortable in my own brain and my own body long before a series of personal traumas took center stage in my life. The big, purpose-driven questions I'd always asked only got louder as things got harder. When chaos ignited right after my 26th birthday, it was like pouring gasoline on a fire that was already flaming hot. The existential questions suddenly felt more urgent.

Existential anxiety isn't necessarily all bad. Like general anxiety, it can be great motivation if you use it as fuel. That's what I've tried to do.

Take this text exchange between me and my business partner, Liv. She's a lot like me—not totally at peace with the past, often anxious about the future and sometimes quick to lose sight of the present. We both know anxiety can drive us, so we approach it that way. Some days, anxiety is the only fuel we have left. It might not be premium, but we'll take it.

Text from Liv: *thoughts on these outfits I just ordered online?*

(Liv sends me a series of photos of various new outfits.)

Text from me: *you look sexy! your ass looks great lol*

Text from Liv: *CoolSculpt and anxiety. Thanksss.*

CoolSculpting, which freezes fat cells to get rid of them, does deserve some airtime of its own, but let's just pause and take a moment for anxiety here. With all the worrying and running around, anxiety can literally whip your ass into shape if you let it. See what I mean? It isn't all bad.

I'm not being insensitive about anxiety's negative effects. Anxiety was one of the many diagnoses I received when I completed an intensive treatment program at the Psychiatric Day Hospital just before my 30th birthday (more on that later). It took three decades, but once I could identify my anxiety, it became less overwhelming.

If you're stuck in your own cycle of anxiety and can't get out, I feel for you. I also want you to know there are healthy ways to channel anxious energy and let it motivate you to take positive action. What if you could experience your anxiety, but also get into action? You don't have to step over your feelings completely, but they also don't have to take you out of the game.

Emotion is just energy in motion—and I suggest you practice using your emotions to move you forward rather than letting them freeze you solid. A CoolSculpting session only lasts 35 minutes. After that, you're off the table, with zero recovery time. Anxiety can be like that, too—and it needs to be if you dream of fulfilling your purpose the way I always did.

If you're anything like me, you've got a bucket list a mile long. You don't like wasting time and you definitely don't want to waste this life. Every now and then, you pause to make sure you're checking off all the boxes, but you also don't want to think about the boxes too much. You want to relax, trust that everything is happening at the perfect time and enjoy these moments you've worked so hard to create. You might meditate, pray and journal, but you still can't stop your brain from skipping timelines and jumping into the future. Future tripping has always been my drug of choice, so you're not alone.

More importantly, you have the power to rewrite your own script. I'm not talking about prescription drugs, though they've proven useful for me at times. I'm talking about the script of your life.

What have I learned from navigating my own major life challenges? If you can figure out how to move through your worry and anxiety, then there's a huge gift waiting for you on the other side. You receive it when you set aside the negative feelings about your own anxiety and figure out how to work with it effectively. This is what rewriting the script looks like. When you do it, you get to glow through what you go through.

Everyone goes through hard times, but not everyone knows they can glow through them, too. When you glow through tragedy, trauma and difficult times, you aren't ignoring what happened. And you don't simply find the silver lining, either. To glow through hard times, you have to become the glow in the dark. You rise up. You get loud. You share your experiences and inspire others. You tell the truth and the truth beyond the truth—or the truth-truth, as I like to call it.

As you glow through what you go through, you may even find a permanent solution to that existential angst. It happened for me. I found my existential cure by getting clear about my purpose and digging my heels into it. Now, when a challenge flares up my existential anxiety and pushes me back to questioning the meaning of life, I dig a little deeper into the work I know I'm meant to do.

In my work, I encourage Inner Glow Circle students to find their purpose and commit to living it. In the process, they often find ways to get paid for work that makes them come alive (and guess what, I made you a free training on this at innerglowcircle.com/training).

An astrologer once told me that the struggles I experienced with my body increased my capacity to get above it, to get perspective. I wouldn't wish my personal hardships on anyone, but I do know that going through the worst four years of my life made me the woman I am today. With the help of many hours in foils at the salon and a major recommitment to clean eating and exercising, I renovated my body and my mind. Rather than coming out of the storm tattered and destroyed, I made it my mission to emerge better than ever—while looking great, too.

SEVEN

GET YOUR GLOW ON

"Just start, and don't worry that you don't have all the answers yet."
—Alli Webb

You don't get a personal guru in life. You have to be your own. You have to wake up every morning ready to follow the breadcrumbs and pay attention to the conversations, experiences, people, places and things that spark your inner glow. You have to take steps toward discovering your purpose so you can find peace in your body and in your brain.

If you don't show up and do that every day, you'll never stop wondering what you're doing here. No one is going to tell you what to do with your life. Existential anxiety requires daily attention from the person who is dealing with it. That means you.

If you're struggling physically, mentally or emotionally, you may feel a fire under your ass to figure out what you're going to do with your life. You might feel a sense of pressure, like you have to take action *now*. It's a cliché, but like most clichés, it's also true. Tomorrow isn't promised. When tragedy hits, your clock starts ticking even faster. Mine sure did.

———

IT TOOK me many years to get diagnosed with Lyme disease. I'm going to tell you all about this in detail later, but for now, I'll just say that it was hard. It killed my dreams of the future. When I lost feeling in my hands, my vision of writing books seemed futile. When the paralysis shot from my foot to my face, numbing the right side of my body, my plans of speaking onstage came to a halt. When I faced the possibility of living life from a wheelchair, my dreams of traveling the world to speak and teach died.

Langston Hughes said, "Hold fast to dreams, for if dreams die, life is a broken-winged bird that cannot fly." I lost my dreams and became that broken-winged bird. I felt sorry for myself. I grieved the life I thought I was supposed to live.

But there's a difference between surrendering and giving up. After years with no answers, I wanted to walk away from everything and play small, but then I realized my dreams didn't have to stop just because I was sick. My body didn't have to set the limits or make the rules. I could dictate my books. I could travel and speak from a wheelchair, couldn't I?

There was only one thing I hated more than being sick: not knowing if I was actually sick or if I was making it all up. I'd lost count of how many doctors had told me that nothing was wrong. I was left doubting myself. Were my body aches, migraines, brain fog and constant chronic pain even real?

After eight years, I got to the bottom of what was *actually* wrong with me. I hadn't been making it up. And as soon as someone tested me, the results were there, clear as day. It had been Lyme disease all along, and it had been caused by a tick bite the summer after I graduated from high school.

You can take illness or any big loss as a fall. You can ride the "why" train for days, months, years. *Why me? Why now?* You can blame yourself in this life or another. *What did I do to deserve this? Am I repaying karma from a past life?* You can get angry at God or the universe for allowing life to be so unfair. *Bad things always happen to me. I can't catch a break.*

But there's an alternative—and I can tell you from experience that it's a better option. You can choose to turn your obstacles into opportunities. I recommend swapping out the constant question of "why" for these more productive alternatives, which I now use whenever I get into a sticky situation:

How can I turn this into an opportunity?
What can I learn from this situation?
What would it look like to go through this and come out stronger?
How can I glow through what I'm going through?

Ask these questions on repeat until the dust settles, the smoke clears and opportunity reveals itself. This is how you begin to glow in the dark and create meaning from whatever mess you're in.

I'm not necessarily the biggest fan of the "If I can do it, you can do it" mantra, but I've found that it *does* help to hear stories of others who have walked through fire and emerged as better versions of themselves. On my journey, the people who spoke to me most were beautiful, powerful women, clearly shaped by tragedy, driven by conviction and guided by purpose. If I can foster a feeling of inner peace and turn my anxiety into action, I think you can, too.

EIGHT

WHEN LIFE GIVES YOU LYME

"Hard days are the best because that's when champions are made."
—Gabby Douglas

"You have mono," the campus nurse said. "It's the kissing disease. It's not serious, but it is spreading around campus."

I had kissed someone at a party that weekend, so I assumed the nurse was right. She handed me five days' worth of antibiotics, and I walked out of the Student Health Center with my head held high.

But after finishing the mono treatment, I didn't feel better. I felt worse. Something wasn't right. My symptoms were consistently random. I had frequent headaches, earaches, stomachaches, repeated sinus infections and neck pain. I had pain down the right side of my body, between my hand and my elbow and in my back and my hip. My feet would go numb. I was tired all the time.

Some days, I had enough energy to run across campus,

hit the gym and make it to my Chi Omega sorority chapter meetings with energy to spare. On other days, I was missing meetings and skipping social activities to stay in bed. I tried to work out, but after I almost fell asleep on the elliptical, I was a little scared.

As you can imagine, my anxiety shot through the roof of my single dorm room as I battled the exhaustion and my many symptoms. All I wanted to do was sleep, but I couldn't put my brain to rest. At night, my mind ran circles around itself and my body ached all over.

Other than the mono, my blood work was perfect, so when I talked about my unrelenting discomfort, it just sounded like complaining. One doctor after another listened to my symptoms and reviewed my blood work. They all said the same thing: "You're fine." When you know something's not fine, but everyone around you keeps saying it is, the only thing left to question is yourself.

The problem was that none of these doctors were thinking outside the box. They suggested it was all in my head, and for a moment, I considered that. But at the end of the day, my body knew.

Everyone is intuitive. What I didn't know back then was that I'm *very* intuitive. I don't just know things—I know *a lot* of things. Ask my friends, the women on our team and our students at Inner Glow Circle. I can often predict the future. I have a strong sense about the past and I definitely know when something isn't adding up in the present. When I get that feeling in my gut, I take action.

At Vanderbilt, I went from bitchin' to mission. I wasn't taking "You're fine" for an answer, especially when I knew it wasn't true. Instead, I went on a hunt to figure out what the hell was wrong with my body.

Meanwhile, my professors weren't as understanding as

I'd hoped. Once, I slept through the alarm for my 8 am Introduction to Communications class. As soon as I woke up, I rolled out of bed in my hot pink sweatsuit and ran across campus to try to catch the last few minutes. At Vanderbilt, it was absolutely unacceptable to wear sweatpants outside your dorm room. On this particular morning, though, I hoped my sweats and no makeup would signal my professor to cut me some slack for being late.

As I arrived at the lecture hall, my class was letting out and the next was filtering in. I was relieved to have made it in time to talk to my professor, but he was not impressed. He said there was no excuse for being late.

I apologized and explained I still hadn't recovered from having mono. I was so tired that I hadn't even heard my alarm! He wasn't having it. Even though I had a doctor's note to prove my case, my professor thought I'd been out dancing on tables until 2 am. At a top university full of rising socialites, this is probably what I *should* have been doing, but I didn't have the energy.

Managing college life at Vanderbilt—the so-called Harvard of the South—was not easy, especially while sick. There were books, boys and a huge focus on outside appearances. When I wasn't able to keep up, the stress in my body multiplied.

I heard Vanderbilt was offering free counseling to undergrads. The sessions were conducted by graduate students in social work. I jumped at the opportunity. This would be my first experience hiring—and very quickly firing—a therapist. It would also be my first piece of evidence in the case I was building against therapy during that time. As far as I could tell, therapy didn't work. Talking to this starter therapist about how bad I felt and how much I was struggling only reinforced my negative feelings.

I was sick and tired of being sick and tired. And I was sick and tired of *talking* about being sick and tired. It was time to go outside the box.

———

WHEN I WENT HOME for winter break, I spilled my secret health challenges to a trusted friend. She told me about a Ukrainian woman who was using Chinese medicine to heal her mom's mystery illness. Even though being poked with tiny needles sounded like further torture, it was worth a shot. Nothing else had worked. I made an appointment and braced myself for an hour of pain. It couldn't be worse than an hour of pretend therapy, right?

I quickly grew to love Dr. Sofiya. Even though she was very vocal about my weight fluctuations, always complimenting or critiquing my changing body, she became my first saving grace.

After running a test I'd never heard of on a machine I'd never seen, Dr. Sofiya told me I had lactose intolerance, gluten sensitivity and something called candida. She said she was concerned, which was more than I'd gotten from any medical professional I'd seen so far. After weekly sessions, some changes to my diet and a few Chinese herbs, we got my symptoms under control. I went back to school, tried not to drink too much and kept in touch about my progress over email.

When I went back to see Dr. Sofiya a few months later during summer break, many of my symptoms had come back. She asked if I wanted to meet with a nutritionist. At this point, acupuncture was the only thing that had given me even a glimpse of relief, and Dr. Sofiya seemed to be the only doctor who was really listening. I would do anything she suggested.

Dr. Sofiya's nutritionist urged me to stop eating gluten and dairy and to drastically cut back on sugar. She explained which foods she believed my body could handle and which ones she felt should be off-limits. The second list was a mile long. There would be no more drinking, no more pasta and no more fro-yo. I accepted that my life was over and followed her directions as closely as possible. I was willing to do anything not to feel sick anymore.

On the path to health, I lost quite a bit of weight. It seemed like the only upside of the whole ordeal. My skin was glowing, too. I returned to school my sophomore year feeling like a better me. My clothes were looser and my skin was brighter. But as soon as I got back to campus and started partying again, my symptoms came back in full force.

The problem remained: I was still sick. Dr. Sofiya had given me some helpful nudges, and if I kept up the acupuncture and perfect diet, it helped. But the pain was still there. I remained an unsolved mystery. No one had figured out what was *really* wrong with me yet. To complicate matters, I not only looked fine, I looked better than ever. *You don't look sick. You've lost weight! Your skin is glowing. At least you look good!* The more I talked about my mystery ailments, the more I got this confusing feedback.

It was annoying to share my experience only to hear people making judgments based purely on the superficial. In an attempt to prove my case, I sometimes tried to *make* myself look sick. If I didn't look good, would doctors stop being blinded by my outside appearance and look deeper?

I stopped getting dressed up and cut back on my makeup routine, but you remember how my professor reacted to that. He didn't. Others didn't seem to react, either. Everyone everywhere still said I looked good. Besides Dr. Sofiya, I couldn't convince anyone of my sickness.

Eventually, I went back to being me—prioritizing beauty and hyper-focusing on looking good. Maybe if I looked good I would feel a little better, too.

Looking good became a coping mechanism. It became the one thing I could control when life felt completely out of my hands.

NINE

SYPHILIS AND A SECOND TEST

"Part of my act is meant to shake you up. It looks like I'm being funny, but I'm reminding you of other things. Life is tough, darling. Life is hard. And we better laugh at everything; otherwise, we're going down the tube."

—Joan Rivers

"Let's get STD tests!"

A few days before we left for senior beach week, I saw a terrifying flyer about STDs in one of my women's studies classes and convinced my friends to take a field trip to Planned Parenthood.

"Let's just go to make sure!"

It seemed like a productive group activity, and as Planned Parenthood was only a few blocks from campus, it didn't really even require a trip. Later, we could all celebrate our STD-free status together.

But that's not what happened.

We were cruising down the highway on the way to Destin, Florida with enough booze to get drunk every night for a month when I got the call. "You tested positive for syphilis," Patricia from Planned Parenthood said. "You need to come in immediately."

"I just left for my senior beach week," I told Patricia. "I won't even be back in Nashville until early next week."

"You need to report here as soon as you get back to Tennessee. If you don't, the state could put out a warrant for your arrest."

WHAT?!

Apparently, it's illegal to transmit an STD, and in Tennessee, it's *even more* illegal. My Catholic guilt took over. Maybe I should have listened when the priest told me sex was a sin. I'd been gearing up for a hell of a week, not a week from hell. *How could this be happening?*

Even though I couldn't understand exactly what was going on, I didn't misunderstand Patricia's tone. She meant business, which scared me even more.

I told her I understood and hung up the phone. Before I could decide whether or not to share the news with my friends, my body decided for me. I burst into tears.

———

OBVIOUSLY, I didn't have much fun during my senior beach week. In the mornings, I lay on the bed while my friends tightened their bikinis in the hotel room mirror and downed tequila shots for breakfast. I fake-laughed and fake-listened, desperately trying to distract myself with their surface-level gossip.

In the afternoons, I lay on the beach, but only to hide under an umbrella with my sunscreen, my confusion and my creeping shame. The only thing scarier than looking at those STD flyers was actually finding out you had one. While the rest of my senior class partied on, hitting their knees for beer bongs and feeling a sense of freedom I no longer felt, I played it safe. I had a few drinks, but there were no shots of Jose Cuervo for me. I worried that if I drank too much, I might hook up with someone and I obviously couldn't do that. I had an STD now.

I felt distinctly *not* young, wild and free as we wrapped up senior beach week and headed back to Nashville. Like a repentant Catholic schoolgirl, I showed up at Planned Parenthood within hours of crossing the state line.

As I finally neared a resolution, a fleeting thought crossed my mind. *Could this be why I've been sick for so long? Have I somehow had syphilis for years?* I hadn't even been that sexually active—but then again, I'd heard you could even get it from a toilet seat.

As soon as I arrived at the clinic, the nurse explained exactly why I was there. They were required to run a second test to verify the first. After such urgency, it felt like a bait and switch to realize they weren't even sure I had syphilis.

This is good news, I thought. *If the test is negative, I'll be able to graduate, get out of here and move on with my life.*

I said a quick Hail Mary or as much of it as I could remember. I wanted God on my side as they ran that second test.

But then I opened my mouth and screwed myself once again.

In my attempt to seem upbeat and *un*manifest the STD I had apparently manifested, I casually mentioned that I was graduating from Vanderbilt and flying home to my parents' house two days later.

"You can't leave Tennessee," the nurse said as she aggressively removed the needle from my arm and sealed the tube on the second blood sample.

"What do you mean I can't leave?"

"You can't leave the state without being treated," she said firmly. "It's illegal. And we won't have the test back in time before you leave. We'll have to treat you today."

"What do you mean 'illegal?'" I asked. "What do you mean 'treat me'?"

The nurse didn't answer. She abruptly left the room.

Until that moment, I hadn't given much thought to what treatment for syphilis would look or feel like. Unlike a lot of STDs, syphilis can't be treated with a pill. Instead, an intramuscular injection of penicillin is required. Imagine sitting on a cold examination table in the back room at a stark Planned Parenthood. The only thing between you and whoever last sat there is a thin sheet of medical exam paper. Your mind is spinning and your anxiety is rising fast. You feel misled by the name of the clinic since nothing about the experience feels planned. After taking your blood sample, a nurse you've only just met walks back into the room, tightly grasping a six-inch shot of milky white penicillin.

"That's huge." The needle is long and the tube is almost an inch thick. "Where's that going?"

The nurse looks at you and tilts her head. Her eyes widen, but she says nothing. She doesn't need to. You've gotten the memo. Your heart speeds up again.

"Go ahead. Turn around and pull your pants down, honey."

You want me to do what?! You think it, but you don't say it out loud. You feel humiliated, but there's no time for emotion. Within seconds, you're bent over the examination table, closing your eyes and gripping the cold, dirty sides with both hands.

The nurse tells you to take a deep breath, so you do. She's got a giant needle in her hand. Of course you're going to follow her directions. "It'll just be a little pinch," she says. She's lying. Over the next 30 seconds, the stinging radiates from your butt cheek through your entire body.

You can take my word for it: Getting treated for syphilis is a total pain in the ass.

Even though the penicillin shot hurt like hell, it was nothing compared to the shame of that needle piercing straight from my skin into my Catholic schoolgirl conscience. Guilt-ridden thoughts ran through my head. *What if my parents find out? My dad will totally disown me and my mom will judge me forever. I can't believe I'm graduating with a bachelor's degree and an STD.*

I pulled up my yoga pants and walked my sore little butt back to campus. What could I do? It was too late to change the situation, and although the treatment wasn't painless, it was fast. My only power was in accepting the past and moving on to a better future.

The next day, I walked across the stage and received my diploma from Vanderbilt. I was proud—and relieved.

Just days after getting pumped with penicillin and graduating from one of the top universities in the country, I boarded a plane, crossed state lines (arrest-free!) and settled back into my parents' house to strategize my next big move.

———

AS I UNPACKED my suitcases in my high school bedroom, my phone rang. It was an unknown Nashville number. *Here we go again,* I thought.

"Is this Miss DePaola?" the man on the other end asked.

As soon as I confirmed my identity, he revealed where he was calling from: Planned Parenthood.

"Miss DePaola, we received the results from your second test."

I took a deep breath.

"It was negative. You don't have syphilis. You never did."

Relief washed over me, followed by anger. I'd spent the last two weeks drowning in guilt and misery for no reason.

As happy as I was to be in the clear, I was pissed about the unnecessary dose of stress—and penicillin—to my already sensitive system. I hadn't been able to enjoy the final weeks of my college experience. What an epic waste.

All the hype had been for nothing, but thank God. Once the anger passed, I could finally exhale. My anxiety levels could return to normal—still high but manageable.

TEN

THE FINAL CLUE

"Sometimes you just have to put on lip gloss and pretend to be psyched."
—Mindy Kaling

After I unpacked my bags at my parents' house, I packed them right back up and moved to New York City.

A year into my life as a New Yorker, I saw a new gynecologist for a standard annual exam. A few days later, I got an anxious message on my voicemail. "We've received your test results," the message said. "Please call the office as soon as possible."

I knew what was coming. I called the office and explained I didn't have syphilis.

"This happened last year," I said.

"We understand," the nurse replied. "You still have to get the second test to be sure. We'll see you tomorrow."

For the next three years, I continued to test positive for

syphilis every time I went to the gynecologist. Eventually, I just started asking for the second test myself.

The syphilis scandal may have been fake news, but my constant sickness was very real. I'd lived seven years with pain, but without answers. So, I turned to acupuncture again. Her name was Meredith. She was not only an acupuncturist, but also a nurse.

———

"I'VE SEEN THIS BEFORE," Meredith said. "Have you ever been tested for Lyme disease?"

"I'm not sure," I told her.

I wasn't sure. I was like a lab rat. I'd had tests run on me for years, but they never told me which ones.

"Lyme is fascinating," Meredith said as she poked my naked body with tiny needles. "People call it the invisible illness because its symptoms make it look like so many other diseases. It can be confused with fibromyalgia, rheumatoid arthritis, even multiple sclerosis. Sometimes people just assume it's a cold that never goes away."

Meredith seemed particularly excited about the topic. Then, she dropped a bomb that suddenly pulled it all together. "You know, people with Lyme often get a false positive result for syphilis."

My stomach dropped. I was silent. There was no way she could have known my history, and I wasn't about to tell her. She paused and poked me with a few more needles.

"Lyme and syphilis are caused by two very similar-looking types of bacteria. A blood test can't always tell the difference."

I said nothing. Lyme sounded scary, and I didn't *want* to

have it. In hindsight, I was too tired to take on the battle, and I still hadn't hit rock bottom yet. I put the conversation out of my mind and kept seeking duct tape solutions. I continued to do all the things I was doing before, but with even more tenacity.

The pain persisted, and all the green juice in the world couldn't save me.

My anxiety was all-consuming. It kept me up at night and took over my days. I tried mindset hacks like meditation, yoga and journaling to try to ease my inner turmoil. I'd sleep for 12 hours, wake up and go right back to bed. My senior year of high school, I was the student government president, homecoming queen and a half marathon-running athlete. Now, at 25, I was a zombie, alive but not really living.

Eventually, my soul started losing steam. I'd lived through years of constant, chronic pain without any answers. I'd been diagnosed with depression, severe dehydration and chronic sinus infections. I was offered sleeping pills, antibiotics and antidepressants. Nothing had worked. What was my next move?

People say that when you ask the universe for a clear sign, the universe answers.

The sign I got was so clear that it catapulted me into action—but first, it nearly paralyzed me.

IN 2013, during my middle brother Johnny's college graduation in Florida, the right side of my body went numb.

For weeks, something had been wrong with my hands. A glass of water slipped from my grasp and shattered across the kitchen floor. My fingers locked up as I tried to dial a phone number. A burning hot cup of tea fell out of my hand and onto my lap.

I may have been trying to ignore my acupuncturist's words about Lyme out of my deep fear of the truth, but that didn't change the fact that I also *desperately* wanted an answer. Finally, I realized that in order to get an answer, I had to face the facts.

If left untreated, Lyme disease can cause paralysis.

In the end, you could say my vanity saved me. When the tingling sensation made its final move from my shoulder to my face, I knew I had to act. I had read that in some cases, facial paralysis was irreversible, and that wasn't okay with me. From the airport in Florida, I made an appointment with a doctor who specialized in treating Lyme.

I can pretend like I was impressed with myself for *finally* making this bold move, but thanks to Meredith and my subsequently late-night Googling, my intuition had been pointing me toward Lyme for over a year. By the time I called that doctor, I was 99 percent sure that Lyme was the culprit.

I would have to wait an entire month for my appointment with the specialist, but as soon as I got home, I got ahead of the game. I went to see my primary care doctor and asked for a Lyme test.

It came back positive. I had Lyme disease.

In the end, it was that simple. All it took was the right test. Now that I knew, I could start to heal, but there was one thing still in my way. All the science I could find agreed on one thing: Lyme did not have a cure.

A month later, I brought the positive test to the Lyme specialist. With a test and a record of my symptoms, it took him just minutes to diagnose me with chronic neurological Lyme disease. This meant it had been untreated in my system for years and caused damage to my brain and other organs. Within a month of my diagnosis, I started treatment.

My doctor said he couldn't heal me, but he promised to help me improve. He was honest about the limitations of his treatment and I appreciated that. But knowing something was wrong and having doctors deny it for nearly 10 years left me questioning everything. *Can I trust my doctors? Can I trust my body? Can I trust myself?*

My mom updated the family via email.

From: Jill Long DePaola
Sent: Wednesday, March 12, 2014 9:27 PM
To: Marlene Long
Subject: Re: Katie update

Just a quick update: Katie has Lyme in her brain, liver and other areas of her body. They feel it has manifested for around 9 years undetected. Although it is in the lower part of the brain, both MRI results showed no lesions in the brain and that is a very good thing. They feel the oral antibiotic treatment as opposed to the intravenous will be the right path for the next 18 months. It is very intense with a lot of drugs, vitamins and antibiotics, quite overwhelming. I feel so very sorry for her that she has been in pain for so long and so long undetected. I think this is a blessing and that we are on the right path now.

My grandma responded.

From: Marlene Long
Sent: Wednesday, March 12, 2014 9:47 PM
To: Jill DePaola
Subject: Re: Katie update

My Katie is so strong and positive that she will get through this with flying colors, plus God is on her side. I love her so much; she has blessed my life.

I prayed that Gram was right—that I was strong enough and positive enough to get through this and that God had my back. Eventually, my protocol would include over 30 pills a day, a cocktail of antibiotics, vitamins and supplements that were meant to kill the Lyme and keep my body strong during the process.

Throughout my treatment, my Lyme doctor continued to remind me that I would never get rid of the disease. The goal was to put it into remission, but it would never go away. He was renowned for his work with Lyme, as well as HIV/AIDS. He'd been published in journals and featured in documentaries, so I believed him.

Treatment was *hard*. Even if pushing past the pain often looked good from the outside, it definitely didn't feel good on the inside. Glowing through my sometimes shitty life required me to make some big choices, the kind that felt really scary at the time.

I had to listen to my body and look beyond medical tests.

I had to keep searching for answers, even when it seemed there were none to be found.

I had to become my own doctor and advocate when traditional doctors failed me.

I had to stay in the game even when every part of me wanted to give up the fight.

These weren't things I was taught to do. They were lessons that revealed themselves after I surrendered to being sick and took on my healing journey.

EVEN AS I STARTED TREATMENT, my career was keeping me busy. I started my first round just weeks before being filmed for a reality television show. Right before I'd hit rock bottom at my brother's graduation, I'd gotten a call from a college friend. She was involved in the filming of an unscripted show based on the lives of a group of women philanthropists in Washington, D.C. Nothing was set in stone, but she thought I'd make a good "character" and wanted to know if I was interested in meeting with someone from the production team about the opportunity. Despite the escalation of my health situation, I went for it. I needed a light at the end of my tunnel.

The best part? The project would start by filming a sizzle reel with a production company that had worked on many *Real Housewives* sets. Admittedly, the show's premise was bad, but my life was worse. If Bethenny Frankel had gotten her start on *The Apprentice: Martha Stewart* just after Stewart's five months in prison, maybe there was hope for me.

I went through a series of interviews, submitted a presentation highlighting the key players in my life and signed a contract saying I wouldn't film with anyone else for the time being. Together, the rest of the cast and I drank champagne and stirred up fake fights for a few weeks. I loved being followed around by a camera.

Unfortunately, when the idea was pitched to major networks, nothing happened. The concept wasn't strong enough to get a pilot. Even though the opportunity never went any further than that initial sizzle reel, the experience became my glow in the dark during this time.

With the show off the table, I wasn't sure what to do

next. What would *you* do if you finally figured out what was wrong with your body after years of searching and suffering —and then found out that your new dream of becoming a reality TV star wasn't going to be the perfect distraction while you healed?

I decided to get a dog, and thank God. Louie would become my loyal companion as my life took even more dramatic turns in the coming years.

Turns out I didn't need a reality show—the drama still found a way to follow me.

———

TRAINING AS A COACH taught me to ask one question: "Is it possible?"

At first, I believed my doctor. I believed Lyme had no cure. But then I started wondering, *"What if he's wrong? What if I don't have to be sick forever? What if I could be healthy again?"*

It takes guts to contradict a doctor who's an expert in his field, who's published in journals and featured in documentaries. But possibility was what initially kept me open to a diagnosis when so many doctors said there was nothing to diagnose. Now I *had* a diagnosis, that according to my doctor, had no cure—but *"Is it possible?"* I asked myself. I followed my doctor's directions and nodded my head at appointments, but at night when I had the energy, I kept researching. I decided to stay quiet but remain open to the chance of a cure.

The first step in creating something new is visualizing it. I created a powerful vision of ultimate health. I wanted to do more than just treat my Lyme. I wanted to be healthier than ever before, so first I had to overcome the limiting belief that I could never be cured. I've always loved proving people wrong. Perhaps this would become another opportunity to do just that.

Limiting beliefs *do* make sense sometimes. They're limited, but believable—that's why they're called limiting beliefs! But just because they make objective sense doesn't mean they're helpful or correct. They're drawn from practicality, not from possibility.

The Lyme treatment was working, but it was rigorous. It wiped me out and made me sick. As the antibiotics killed the disease, my body was flooded with toxins and my brain fog and memory loss got worse. I started writing everything down: what happened that day, how I was feeling, what helped my symptoms and what seemed to make them worse. I tracked everything, and as I did, I started paying *very* close attention.

Listening to my body allowed me to start trusting myself more than ever before. My body had been right the whole time, so I continued to listen diligently. If something helped me feel even one percent better, I made note of it. By tracking what made me feel better, I could isolate solutions and zoom in on what worked.

———

IT WOULD TAKE three more years, two more Lyme doctors and various treatment protocols, but ultimately, I did what once seemed impossible. I cured my Lyme. Along the way, I became an expert in self-care. I made it my mission to look good—and to feel good, too.

In the "looking good" category were things like getting spray tans, putting on fake eyelashes, getting my hair done and dressing in a way that made me feel sexy and alive.

Now and then, I bought some fresh lingerie and did a bit of redecorating to spruce up my space.

In the "feeling good" category were things like eating healthy, drinking green juice, making gratitude lists, saying affirmations, getting acupuncture, going to yoga, following my intuition, buying myself flowers, painting, lighting candles and spending time outside.

Certain things like drinking less, exercising more, getting good sleep and cutting back on sugar seemed to do both. I may have been sick, but I was learning to glow from the inside out—and from the outside in. It didn't seem to matter whether I was focused on how I felt or how I looked. I was focused on myself and on my healing. All of it made a positive difference. I was manifesting my way to ultimate health.

ELEVEN

THE SELF-CARE SCANDAL

"Caring for myself is not self-indulgence, it is self-preservation, and that is an act of political warfare."
—Audre Lorde

At the height of my "Lyme-is-the-reason-for-all-my-suffering" era—when I barely left my 450-square-foot apartment in D.C. and had almost everything I needed delivered via an app—I attributed all my physical, mental and emotional pain to my diagnosis. During that period, my anxiety was all-consuming. I couldn't leave my apartment because I *couldn't* physically leave my apartment. I met with my coaching clients over the phone, often from my bed with the lights turned off. My super professional website and the pictures from my new photo shoot (which took place in my home, obviously) looked good, but they were hiding a whole lot of shit—aka the truth-truth.

As I got sicker with Lyme, though, it got harder and harder to keep up appearances. And as my body slowed down, my mind sped up, trying desperately to take control and work through the pain on its own.

Today, I believe the self-care obsession I developed in my early 20s stemmed from my deep desire to fix what was going wrong with my body. I grew up in a family of fixers. We handled things ourselves. If it was too much to deal with or we didn't know how, we hid our problems for as long as we could.

I didn't know it then, of course, but when I moved to New York, I was four years into my battle with Lyme. Since my health issues were still an unsolved mystery, taking my self-care to the next level seemed like the appropriate solution. The problem was that in my world, self-care was an *act*, not an actual way of living. I kept the act up for a long time.

I became so good at acting like I was taking care of myself that it shouldn't have come as a surprise that I heard some variation of "At least you look good!" whenever I'd share my physical and emotional challenges.

In my family, looking good has always been a priority. It wasn't that no one cared how you felt. It was just that you were *supposed* to feel good, so it was assumed you did. During the years I didn't feel well and didn't know why, the only place left to look was the mirror. *There must be something wrong with me,* I thought on repeat.

In hindsight, I have to wonder if hyper-focusing on self-care during this period kept me from seeing I had Lyme all along. If self-care hadn't been splattered across the cover of every magazine I saw, would I have listened to my nurse-acupuncturist when she more or less diagnosed me? Could there have been other doctors, nurses and healers who mentioned Lyme to me along the way, but I just didn't hear it? Did I accept looking good and feeling bad as the best it could get for me? Sure, it took doctors almost 10 years to diagnose me, but it also took me 10 years to diagnose myself.

THERE'S nothing intrinsically *wrong* with self-care. I sell it myself through my work at Inner Glow Circle. It's just not a full solution to most ailments, and in my opinion, it's often marketed as a cure-all. That's why I call it a scandal. The way to outsmart any scandal is to understand it, and my personal understanding comes from my own experience.

Desperate for answers, I tracked and then repeated anything that made me feel better, but eventually my self-care Band-Aids were no longer cutting it. I was more miserable than ever. Besides my physical pain, I was in emotional turmoil. I showed up to work one day and couldn't force myself to pick up the phone and call the leads at my start-up sales job. Other than the nonprofit board I was on for an organization that mentored underserved teen girls, nothing in my life had a purpose. I had a boyfriend I'd met at work, but he was leaving the job and I wanted to quit, too. I felt unfulfilled.

Shortly after the day I refused to call another lead at my sales job, I quit. Then I moved closer to home. Even though healthy food spots were much harder to find in Washington, D.C., my obsession with self-care continued—but this time, I went deeper than just the surface.

"SPEND your Tuesday evenings reconnecting with your inner artist, taking action toward your ideal life and relishing in a supportive circle of like-minded women.

During our gatherings we will participate in artistic ventures, set creative goals and emerge a little more playful while incorporating a dollop of yoga, meditation and journaling."

This was the description of a seven-week class called the Creativity Circle and taught by Kimberly, the owner of my new yoga studio in D.C. Kimberly also happened to be a published author and an entrepreneur. When I heard about this class, I thought it might be the key to a new me—a me who *actually* cared about myself and didn't just play the self-care game. With a healthy dose of skepticism, I signed up. I had nothing to lose.

Until this point, everything I'd spent money on in the self-care space was connected to my *outer* self. Besides taking an $85 vision board workshop in New York City, reading $20 books by Gabby Bernstein and meeting famed feminist Erica Jong at the writing retreat my then-boss paid for, I hadn't invested in much inner work. I didn't even have a therapist.

The creativity class was $360, which was much more than a new lipstick, a full-body massage or even a new outfit. When I think about the tens of thousands of dollars I've dropped on my personal development since, it seems silly that I was worried about a few hundred, but I had never invested in my inner self. This was a new way to spend on self-care.

As a supplement to the Creativity Circle, we were asked to read *The Artist's Way*, a book meant to facilitate what Kimberly called a "creative recovery." She told our class that she credited the book with the launch of her yoga studio and her entrepreneurial career. That sounded hopeful. If a book could help me find myself, figure out what I wanted to do with my life and find answers to the overwhelming questions that had surfaced since I left New York, I was in.

Guess what? The class worked. The experience got me out of my comfort zone during the very first session. That night, I set aside my glue stick and magazines and nervously got up to go to the bathroom, which was located in the back of the tiny yoga room. I *thought* I'd heard the lock click when I closed the sliding door, but I was so anxious about disturbing the class that I must have skipped that step.

Mid-pee, I heard the door sliding open. I would have pulled it shut, but it was completely out of reach. If being vulnerable was key to the creativity process, I was becoming a star student without even trying.

Embarrassment wasn't the only path out of my comfort zone. I was also challenged by the course itself, particularly the work I was asked to do outside the lavender-infused "classroom." As homework, I was required to start writing what *The Artist's Way* calls Morning Pages. It was journaling, but with a few added rules. First, I had to write as soon as I woke up. Second, I had to write by hand. Third, I couldn't stop until I got to three full pages. The fourth step wasn't possible until I got through 12 whole weeks of writing. At that point, I would have to go back and highlight in two different colors—one color for insights and another for actions to take.

When it came to Morning Pages, clarity was the ultimate goal. They took time—about 30 minutes a day—but were so impactful that they ultimately created *more* time. Clarity made prioritization easy, which freed up space in my days. I'd been journaling for most of my life, but in the past, I would only write as much as I felt like writing, which often meant I was stopping after half a page. With this practice, I had to keep going.

According to Julia Cameron, author of *The Artist's Way*, "Each morning, as you face the page, you meet yourself. The pages give us a place to vent and a place to dream. They are intended for no eyes but our own."

I took the whole process very seriously. If Cameron said writing three pages a day would help me tap into my inner creativity and maybe even find my purpose in life, I was going to write three pages a day. Now and then, mysteriously, my fingers would lose feeling and lock up on me. I wrote through the pain. It was cathartic and clarifying.

Eventually, writing in this way pushed me to identify the parts of my life that were no longer working and uncover the deeper desires I'd spent decades pushing down. When I went back to highlight the insights and actions, I magically had a plan for the next six months.

When you write with consistency, you start to see your own neuroses. You see the ways that you hold yourself back. You see how many of your childhood desires never went away. They just got pushed so far down your priority list that you almost forgot about them.

The Creativity Circle gave me the inspiration I was desperately craving. It also lit a fire under my ass. I promised myself I wasn't going to waste any more of my life doing things I didn't really love. Between learning alongside like-minded women, consistently writing and tapping into my artistic side, my life was changing at a rapid pace. As I paid closer attention to my desires and my days, I noticed more and more synchronicities. Prioritizing my inner self-care was paying off.

Being sick for a long time had messed with my head, but even before that, I didn't have a very strong vocabulary around my emotions. My family rarely talked about their feelings, so I didn't have a ton of awareness around mine, either. I didn't know how I felt from one moment to the next, and I had no idea how to figure it out. This chapter in my life helped me discover a deeper layer within. For once, I could stop feeling so alone in my anxiety, existential and otherwise. I wasn't the only one seeking purpose and meaning. There were others—and they were sitting right in that creativity class, seeing me pee.

TWELVE
A SELF-CARE SOLUTION

"You may encounter many defeats, but you must not be defeated. In fact, it may be necessary to encounter the defeats, so you can know who you are, what you can rise from, how you can still come out of it."

—Maya Angelou

If you'd asked me to define self-care as a 25-year-old life coach, I would have gone on some tangent about buying yourself flowers, investing in massages and drinking wine (but not too *much* wine) in your pajamas. I might have even added something about vision boards and journaling. After the Creativity Circle class, I would have mentioned *The Artist's Way,* making time to be creative and those Morning Pages.

If you asked if self-care also included setting healthy boundaries, going to therapy and taking time off from work, I would have stared at you blankly.

These days, I know you can't outsource your self-care. It's a way of being, not a single transaction, and you definitely can't buy it at the beauty counter, no matter how many times you try. Effective self-care requires you to actually be caring toward yourself, and at 25, I didn't know how to do that. Back then, instead of learning how to fill my own cup, I let other people do all the pouring. They often missed the glass completely.

You can't treat an anxiety disorder with a hot yoga class, and you can't cure depression with a bouquet of fresh flowers and a green juice. I've tried. As I said earlier, self-care isn't a cure-all.

It wasn't my fault that I'd misinterpreted it that way. Society sells self-care. It's one of the biggest scandals impacting women today. Women are constantly being sold the latest trends in nail shapes, body wraps and weekend getaways as *essential* self-care. It's all a big lie, and it's pretty harmful if you ask me. In 2014, the year I got diagnosed with Lyme, self-care was a $10 billion industry. In 2020, it boomed to $450 billion. Add in "wellness" and you're into the trillions.

If you've gotten seduced by the clickbait titles on your favorite sites, you're not alone: *9 Ways to Practice Self-Care on a Budget. 12 Surprising Things You Never Knew Could Count as Self-Care. 35 Self-Care Tips You Can Try Even If You're Living on the Moon.* You've probably even taken some online quiz about the best type of self-care for your personality or what you would *be* if you were a kind of self-care.

It took me forever to understand that self-care actually meant caring for myself based on what I needed—not only physically, but also mentally and emotionally—and not based on what social media, blogs and magazines told me I needed. I was doing all the things wellness experts tell you to do, but I wasn't caring for myself in a real way because I didn't know how to yet.

Instead of actually taking care of myself and making tangible life changes to show some real self-love (like letting go of friendships I'd outgrown, leaving my job and taking an actual vacation), I tried to spot-treat the whole thing. Massage this week. Acupuncture next week. Manicures and pedicures as needed. Therapy, never. I was still hung up on the lame therapy experience I'd had back at Vanderbilt. Plus, I didn't want to dwell on the past. I wanted to move confidently into the future.

TO START BEING *self-care instead of just* doing *self-care so that I can actually live my purpose.*

This was the objective I wrote for myself in the year-long coaching program my creativity class breakthroughs inspired me to enter. We were asked to design project plans based on the areas where we wanted to grow—and work those plans throughout the year. They were like mini business plans, but for life.

Even though I'd gotten better at prioritizing myself, I still compromised my own needs in almost every relationship, especially romantic ones. Worst of all, I still didn't feel happy. I was uncovering big dreams for my life and my future, but they didn't mean a thing without a sufficient level of emotional wellness and baseline stability. If I couldn't change myself, how could I change the world?

I started by creating this self-care plan.

"What do you mean you need more self-care? You look

great!" This was my classmate's response when I showed her my plan.

There it was again. *At least you look good.* I explained to her that the fact that I looked good—but still didn't feel good—was precisely why I needed to do the project.

"That makes sense," she said. "But how will you measure your results?"

It was a fair question. When creating an objective for a project plan, most people set a quantifiable goal based on money or numbers. How was I supposed to measure my new embodiment of self-care?

It could only be measured in one way: according to how I felt.

As soon as I got into the feelings territory, my resistance ran wild. *Why am I doing this? My self-care is fine. I just need to go to bed earlier.* I considered scrapping the project altogether and choosing a more business-oriented goal. But I couldn't give up.

My classmate's reaction suggested that looking good was a signal that my self-care cup was full, but I know from experience this wasn't the case. So, I made it my mission to show the world that idea was incomplete. Looking good and feeling good are not one and the same.

More motivated than ever by my classmate's initial response, I took the project to my coach, who was mentoring me through my coach training certification. She asked what *being* self-care looked like to me, and I finally found an answer.

Real self-care involved less bubble baths and more boundaries, more fun and less stress. It was about taking time off, not figuring out how to be more "on." My performance was always on point, which was why I had everyone fooled. My rest time? Non-existent. Based on these realizations, I updated my list of self-care activities.

Eat healthy meals throughout the day.

Be in bed by ten on weeknights.

Say no when I want to say no.

Stop working on the weekends.

Stop working after 8 pm.

Take a vacation once per quarter.

"Is a relationship part of that equation?" my coach asked after reviewing the list. "Would that feel like self-care?"

Yes, letting myself be in a healthy relationship would be very self-caring. Allowing myself to want a real relationship, instead of the quick flings I'd been having with one guy after another, was an act of self-care I'd been avoiding. I wanted to be in love and it was time to admit it, but I didn't see how I could make space for a real relationship without compromising my other priorities.

My old beliefs about self-care made me think that taking care of myself was in opposition to taking care of everything else. If I prioritized myself first, I was pushing my business, clients, family and friends down on the list.

I was used to squeezing in self-care, rather than gracefully weaving it through my entire life. In the old approach, makeup, long baths, healthy foods, girls' nights and writing for a few minutes in my journal meant I loved myself. The new story meant I had to deal with my emotions, talk about my feelings, work toward creating a life I loved and actually be open to real love. I added more to my list, hoping it wasn't in opposition to everything else:

Be in a loving relationship.

Go for my dreams.

Value my commitments.

Be open about my feelings.
Take baths.

Yes, baths got to stay. It's not like surface-level self-care is *bad* for you. A lot of creative magic can happen in the bathtub! But it's not limited to the bathtub, either.

With my expanded list, I was almost finished defining the project. My coach asked me to dig deeper.

"What are these things on your list in service of?" she asked. "What's possible if you go to bed earlier?"

"I can wake up early to do morning meditations and do more freewriting so I can work on my book."

With that answer, I got my coach's point. Every piece of my self-care project was meant to support something bigger. Writing my first book (the one you have in your hands), getting into the right relationship and leaving the jobs that kept me from my purpose, so I could focus on it fully, were key aspects of successful self-care. I had to be willing to let my old life go so I could make room for a new one.

A month later, I started writing my book. I was wrapping up work by 8 pm and going to bed early just as I said I would.

If the first half of 2013 was about self-care, the second half was about self-discovery. There were ups and downs, but looking back now, it was one of the most expansive years of my life. It was the year I became a trained coach, met my current business partner and began to make real money through coaching. It was also the year I started to truly care for myself.

I didn't know it then, but it was also the year I'd fall for my future ex-fiancé, find out I had Lyme and understand the turmoil my youngest brother was experiencing more fully.

THIRTEEN

WHAT I LEARNED FROM LYME

"Life keeps throwing me stones. And I keep finding the diamonds."
   —Ana Claudia Antunes

Today, I'll tell anyone anything about me. This hasn't always been the case. The decade I spent sick turned me into a pretty private person. I didn't want to scare people with my sickness or my symptoms. I didn't want clients to stop signing up to work with me. I didn't want my team to be afraid I'd disappear. I didn't want my family, friends or boyfriends to ask too many questions. I didn't want to get labeled as the sick girl who was fun, but flaky—even though for many years, I was just that.

In the beginning, few people knew about my struggle with Lyme, and those who did didn't really get it. How could they? If you tell someone you have a cold, they get it, because if they're a living, breathing human who's ever left the house, they've likely had a cold before. Try telling someone you have an invisible illness and the symptoms are a mix of severe seasonal allergies, the worst hangover of your life, multiple nights of sleep deprivation and debilitating anxiety. It's a lot to grasp if you haven't experienced it yourself.

Separately, none of those symptoms seem *that* bad, and since a lot of them sound like a common cold, people *think* they can empathize. Who hasn't had a bout of anxiety or a sleepless night? But I hated when people acted like they knew what I was feeling. It was one of the worst parts of living with a chronic illness.

Thanks to thousands of hours spent listening to humans tell their stories in my work as a coach and now, a trainer of coaches, I've learned that this is how it goes for pretty much every major life experience. Lyme may be known as an invisible illness, but all pain is invisible in its own way. The only way to understand it is by going through it.

Today, I see my experience with chronic illness as a metaphor, a lesson about all kinds of pain. There was so much going on with me that no one could see. I didn't *look* sick, but the tick bite I got during that summer after high school caused destructive bacteria to take over my body and my brain. No one knew how terrible I felt at the height of my battle with Lyme or how many nights I prayed not to wake up in the morning because the physical and emotional pain was so debilitating. No one knew the extent of my depression or how much my anxiety was running my life. How could they? I kept quiet. I tried not to complain.

I didn't think I was supposed to talk about my pain. To the outside world, I was a well-dressed, makeup-wearing, privileged white girl who generally looked good. I still hoped that someday the looking good would translate into feeling good.

Lyme wasn't the only part of my life that looked one way but felt another. While our family seemed picture-perfect on the outside, my youngest brother was struggling with a dual diagnosis: bipolar illness and addiction.

And then there was the relationship with my then-fiancé. Although people would stare with envy and girls would stop me at brunch to comment on my seven-carat cushion cut diamond ring, it was all a facade. The ring was so big and sparkly that people assumed my relationship was big and sparkly, too. In reality, it was all fake—and I still wonder about the ring. The GIA certificate said it was real, but you can forge anything these days, can't you?

I know you have secrets. You were trained to keep them —by your parents, your friends, the culture you grew up in. Even the influencers you follow online have secrets, and by not sharing them, they're encouraging you to stay quiet, too. Shame is the name of the game.

No one totally gets you. No one knows your wounds. Ultimately, that's why you've been trying to operate on *top* of everything you experience. You've been trying to keep going. *No one's going to get it anyway,* you think.

I'm here to tell you that I get it. Thanks to our shame culture, I know that sometimes you don't feel fine, even if you insist you do.

I don't pretend to understand your exact situation. There's no way for me to know exactly what it feels like to be you. *I'm not you.* But that's precisely the part I get. I get that you're you and I'm me and neither of us is living pain-free, because life, in essence, involves pain.

Lyme taught me this: Pain, no matter how invisible, is real. If you want to glow through what you go through, you have to start by knowing that what you're experiencing is real.

FOURTEEN

MANIFESTATION AND PARTIAL HOSPITALIZATION

"I understand now that I'm not a mess, but a deeply feeling person in a messy world."
—Glennon Doyle

What you're experiencing is real, but you can still get stuck in your head.

Both the Law of Attraction and the concept of manifestation are based on one simple idea: Change your thoughts and you'll change your life. After years of grief, I wanted to believe it was that simple. I read more about manifestation and visualization, took courses and listened to coaches and leaders in the spiritual self-help world.

During my personal trifecta of disease, death and the breakup that felt like a divorce, I worked with two Lyme specialists, two naturopaths, a psychiatrist, seven therapists, three acupuncturists and so many coaches, psychics and astrologers that I lost count. All but one told me that the Lyme would never go away. It wasn't until I considered the possibility myself that the doctor who could heal me would arrive.

One day I realized that part of the problem was that I couldn't envision myself as a healthy person. In 10 years, I never once took the time to sit down and let myself experience the feeling of being well. I never asked myself, *"What will it feel like to be well again? What emotions will I experience when I am fully healthy?"* I said I wanted it, but I never visualized myself with ultimate health.

The other problem, though, was that my trauma was blocking my vision. It didn't matter how hard I tried, how many affirmations I said or how many gratitude lists I wrote. My head was still flooded with negativity and my body felt an overwhelming sense of doom.

When the phone rang, I worried it would be life-shattering news, like the call I got the day my brother died. When I opened my email, I worried there'd be another threatening email from my ex, like the ones I took to the courthouse to get a protective order against him. They were irrational fears to some extent, but they were also rational, because they were based on things that had happened. When I looked at the spot on the wall in my kitchen where my ex had punched a hole, I'd still see a hole, even though it had been repaired months before. I would close my eyes and see flashes of my brother in his casket.

The flashbacks became overwhelming. It would take some time for me to do enough research to understand that all the mindset work in the world wouldn't cure my PTSD. And PTSD was exactly what I had.

Trying to heal my trauma through manifestation was the equivalent of trying to cure my Lyme through self-care. No matter how much I meditated, how clearly I visualized or how many affirmations I repeated out loud, I was drowning and I couldn't find my way to the surface. I couldn't experience pleasure. I was either in pain or I was numb.

When I started to sense the numbness, I knew it was time to test myself, to see what I might be able to feel. I spent time with good men—and some not-so-good men. I got a few tattoos. I overworked myself and then didn't work at all. I continued to feel nothing.

"I CAN'T DO THIS ANYMORE," I said.

"What do you mean, Katie?" my parents asked in sync.

"I literally can't handle my life." My voice was trembling. "I need to go to the hospital."

I'd experienced panic attacks before, but this one was different. I felt so much weight on my shoulders that I couldn't stand up straight. All I could hear was my heartbeat. My breath was rapid. I tried to calm down, but I couldn't.

"Come to the house and I'll take you," my dad said.

The night before, a loud banging woke me just as I was falling asleep. My heart raced. My mind flashed to my ex. *Could that be him?* I wondered as I lay in the dark. It had been a year since I'd seen him in court and months since he'd signed the papers releasing my company back to me.

As it turned out, the banging was the police responding to a false alarm next door, but it didn't feel false to my body. I didn't sleep at all that night. By morning, I was in the midst of a full-blown panic attack. The experience had triggered unresolved memories that I hadn't fully dealt with.

In the lobby of the emergency room, I alternated between panicking and being totally checked out. My body shook. My head was pounding. My pupils were dilated. I felt agitated by everyone and everything. I was sweating through my clothes. After waiting for hours, the doctor came in and asked for my medical history. I told him I was being treated for Lyme.

He diagnosed me with a migraine and discharged me with no further explanation. I went home and slept.

The next day, searching for an explanation for my recent trip, I called my therapist. After all that trialing, I'd finally found someone I liked and had been working with for months. She was curious about the hospital visit and brought up my recent appointment with a new psychiatrist.

"Did she prescribe you any medication?" she asked.

"Celexa." I'd taken it before. My first Lyme doctor had prescribed it when the treatment was taking the wind out of my sails.

"How have you been feeling since you started on it?"

"Really weird, actually."

The therapist asked how long the psychiatrist talked to me before she wrote the prescription, whether I was seeing any other doctors and if I was taking other supplements. She wondered if my symptoms had been caused or at least aggravated by the antidepressant.

I closed my eyes and remembered the appointment. At 29 years old, it was my first session with a psychiatrist.

We talked for 45 minutes. She asked if I'd ever taken any medication for my anxiety. When I mentioned Celexa, she had only one question.

"Did you have any side effects?"

"I have no idea," I told her. "I was taking 30 pills and supplements a day back then. I felt horrible all the time. I even blacked out once during treatment, but I don't know what caused it."

My psychiatrist handed me a new prescription for the same drug, but she missed one glaring issue: dual treatment.

A few months prior, on my 29th birthday, I'd flown to Tampa to celebrate with Liv. I'd been stable and in remission for a year and I wasn't worried. We had a full spa day that included an intense steam room session. The next morning, I woke up dizzy, delirious and drenched in sweat. I knew instantly that the Lyme was back. After over a year of high dose antibiotics, all it took was damp heat to reactivate the Lyme that was dormant in my system. When I got home, I found a new doctor, a naturopath who put me on a different Lyme protocol and began his own course of treatment for my anxiety. There was another Lyme specialist he wanted me to see, but his waitlist was months long. In the meantime, this naturopath would treat me.

I mentioned my naturopath to the psychiatrist, but since his protocol consisted of supplements and herbal tinctures, she said she wasn't concerned about interactions. She wrote the Celexa prescription and urged me to start taking it right away.

In response to this update, my therapist said, "Did your naturopath give you a supplement called 5-HTP?"

I grabbed my vitamin stash and confirmed I'd been taking 5-HTP for months.

"Oh my God! You had serotonin syndrome. I've heard of it, but I've never seen it happen." My therapist solved the ER case.

Serotonin syndrome is essentially a serotonin overdose, caused by the use of two or more medications that increase serotonin. While serotonin is known for creating happy feelings in the body, it *is* possible to have too much of a good thing.

After I regained the color in my face post-serotonin trip,

I called the psychiatrist who had more or less caused my visit to the emergency room. I told her what my therapist had discovered and asked why 5-HTP hadn't come up in our conversation.

"Listen, Katie. You have *a lot* going on," she said. "Between the Lyme and everything else you've been through over the past few years, it's hard to decipher what's what. I think you should look into a PHP program."

I didn't know what that meant.

"A partial hospitalization program," she clarified.

"That sounds *really* serious." I laughed out loud at the idea. Visions of cold, stark mental hospitals flooded my mind.

"They're just day programs, and your situation *is* serious. Do some research and consider it."

A few hours later, I found myself sitting in my car, in my parents' driveway, talking to God.

"Why am I still struggling?"

And this was my breakthrough realization: I hadn't decided to heal.

———

ALTHOUGH MANIFESTING ISN'T A CURE-ALL, I've learned how to use it to speed up my healing journey. It's important to know that manifesting isn't just about making a vision board with hot couples and honeymoon sunsets and hoping "the one" will show up. You have to go through an intentional process of visualizing what you want, understanding who you need to become to have it and doing the things that version of you would do. If I say I want to make hundreds of millions of dollars in my business, be an influential philanthropist or be on a certain TV show, I have to ask myself if I'm showing up *now* as the philanthropist multimillionaire on TV.

Today, I teach my own process, 5 *Steps to Manifesting* (get the free workshop at innerglowcircle.com/manifesting). At its core, manifesting is about *creating* with intention. It can't be haphazard if you want it to work. The process I teach has five steps: seeing, feeling, being, doing and having. I developed this process as I was trying to understand why manifesting didn't work for me. Maybe what I was missing is what you've been missing, too.

First, you have to *see* what you want, which includes envisioning it. Get clear on what you want and go into as much detail as possible. Close your eyes and imagine. Write what you see. You can even make a vision board to create a detailed visual of what you desire. Ask yourself: *What do I want?*

Second, you have to *feel* the feelings that come along with having what you want before you actually have it in physical form. This is the best integrity check to make sure what you're focused on is what you truly want—and not just what you *think* you want, what you used to want or what someone else wants for you. If the feelings you imagine include gratitude, excitement and expansion, you're on the right track. Ask yourself: *How will I feel when I have what I want?*

Third, you have to look at who you need to be as a person to have what you want to have. This is where you get yourself ready to have the thing you want. It's also where the Law of Attraction comes into play. You have to start to become the person who has what you desire. It's about evolving yourself from the inside out, and it's the most intricate step of my manifesting process because it requires you to become your future self *now*. Ask yourself: *How would the version of me who already has what I want be in the world? How would they live, work and play? How would they walk, talk, eat or exercise? How would they show up?*

When you ask these questions, you start to see where you're not yet being the person you say you want to be. It's an integrity check, so be honest with yourself about the reasons you don't fully want what you say you want or the reasons you're afraid to have it. If, for example, you say you want to be healthy, and the version of you who's healthier would be eating clean and exercising while the current version of you is watching Netflix on the couch, you have to get real about that. If you say you want to be on TV, but you're not even making YouTube videos, it's time to check yourself. The key to manifesting is in this third step right here—finding ways to become your future self now.

Fourth, you have to do what your future self would do. Once you have all this clarity and direction from the first three steps, you have to get into action. Write a list of everything someone who has what you want might do. The key is to start doing what your future self needs you to do before you're ready, because "ready" is a lie. Consider the version of you who has what you want. Ask yourself: *What would they do?*

In the fifth and final step, you embrace having what you wanted all along. Once you've gone through the first four steps, what you want usually shows up.

How can you continue to welcome the fruits of your labor into your life? If what you said you want hasn't manifested, you have to go back and reevaluate. Was there a part of you that didn't want what you said you wanted? Was there a part of you that was afraid to have it?

When it comes to manifesting, the biggest mistake people make is trying to jump from seeing to having without laying the groundwork along the way. It's not that you can't manifest what you want quickly—but you do have to be conscious of the steps required to get there. If you want a healthy relationship, you have to start doing the things someone in a healthy relationship would do, like communicating openly, being vulnerable and going on dates. There are always steps along the way.

How do you create the life you want when you've been through total chaos? You find the glow in the dark—but *you* have to light the candle yourself. It doesn't happen on its own. The past is over, but the future is waiting for you to write it.

FIFTEEN

THE AWAKENING

"Each night, when I go to sleep, I die. And the next
morning, when I wake up, I am reborn."
—Mahatma Gandhi

After my trip to the emergency room, I called in backup. I
spoke to Liv, my business partner, and told her I needed to
take some time off. I told her my Lyme had hit an all-time
low and that my head was all messed up (which she was
probably relieved to hear me admit). My memory was shit. I
was constantly anxious and distracted. None of this was
news to her. You can tell when someone close to you is
losing steam.

I left out the part about the partial hospitalization
program. I was embarrassed and didn't want Liv to think I'd
completely lost my mind. She told me she'd handle things at
work and to take care of myself.

I spent the next week calling various mental health
facilities in search of an opening. The one that was closest

to my parents' house called me back. They had space for me. My body relaxed when I got the news. I was told to come in for an interview with the program director to see if I would be a good match. It was like the college admissions process all over again. I'd finally accepted that I needed real help. Now I wanted to pass the interview and get in.

That weekend, I went to the beach with my parents. I made the mistake of asking for their *opinions* about the partial hospitalization program rather than their support.

"Bo was supposed to go through a similar program," my mom said. "But he wouldn't go."

"Bo needed this kind of program, but you don't," Dad chimed in. "You're focused and successful. Why don't you just come live with us for a few months?"

Everything in my body said no, but I looked at my mom for an answer.

"I'll support whatever you choose," she said.

I was quiet for a minute. Then I said, "Guys, I'm going. I'll go for Bo, too."

AS SOON AS I committed fully, miracles started to pour in. I was interviewed and accepted. My first official day was a Friday. The psychiatric assistant who opened the day told me a big group had just finished the program. I was the only patient for now and would receive one-on-one treatment until more people arrived. The head therapist apologized for the lack of group experience for the time being. After the past few years, nothing sounded more luxurious than a few days of one-on-one analysis. I felt like I had just landed a spot at Canyon Ranch.

Within 72 hours, I was diagnosed with generalized

anxiety disorder, major depressive disorder, post-traumatic stress disorder and obsessive-compulsive disorder.

The PTSD, they said, was the biggest culprit, because it was making all my other tendencies worse. I'd heard about the disorder in reference to war veterans, but I didn't realize that I'd fought through psychological warfare myself. I had all the symptoms to prove it: irritability, hypervigilance, difficulty concentrating, heightened sensitivity to being startled, shaking and a general feeling of detachment. Coupled with the serotonin overdose, I now understood why the banging next door had set off such a panicked response in my system.

The OCD diagnosis came when the program's art therapist asked me to draw a house. At this point, three other people had joined the class, including a cancer survivor who'd become addicted to medication she was given during treatment and a man in his 50s who spent the entire class complaining about his parents not letting him do what he wanted. My drawing was the most detailed of the group. It included a detailed lawn with a detailed tree and detailed bushes. I sketched out leaves and blades of grass. I added perfectly installed windows and a roof with shingles. As I focused on standardizing the shingles, making them the same shape and size, the art therapist came and stood behind me. I tried to explain that my family had a remodeling business.

"I just know my way around a house," I said.

"Mmmm, I think it's more than that! I see a little OCD in here!"

My art therapist's excitement reminded me of my acupuncturist's reaction when she first suggested I might have Lyme. I get it now. A diagnosis can be quite exciting.

JUST TWO DAYS after starting the partial hospitalization program, I got a call from the Lyme doctor who had put me on a nine-month waitlist. But it hadn't been nine months. It hadn't even been nine weeks. Apparently, the God who was talking to me in the car that day had also been listening when I said I was running out of time.

The following week, I took a day off from partial hospitalization to see the doctor. This would be my third round of Lyme treatment and roughly the 30th person I'd seen to try to solve my medical mystery. He confirmed my case was serious and we started weekly treatments. He couldn't promise a timeline, but he felt he could cure it.

No one had *ever* told me Lyme could be cured until this doctor did.

Maybe it was the power of prayer or maybe I was finally getting honest about the fact that I was operating with one foot in and one foot out of my own life. Maybe it was the new care I was showing for my mental health that opened the door for me to experience transformation in my physical health. Maybe it was the actions I took after the breakdown in my parents' driveway, asking everyone and their mom if they knew the doctor I wanted to see—and when I got a list of three people who did, begging them to call and tell him my story. It was the medical version of "Can you put in a good word for me?" Whatever the reason, my nine-month timeline toward healing had collapsed into a few weeks. I was on my way to a cure.

BY MY 30TH birthday that September, I was Lyme-free. It was a bigger miracle than I ever could have imagined. Everyone said it would never happen, and it wasn't until I had the radical, radical thought that even though 30 doctors didn't have a cure, I could still meet the one who did.

I still believe in miracles. I also think mindset work and manifestation can go hand in hand with therapy, coaching and other healing modalities that teach you how to redirect your thought patterns.

I'm embarrassed to tell you how much money I spent on coaches, therapists and spiritual teachers between the moment I lost feeling in my body at the end of 2013 and finally getting cured in the fall of 2017. These people urged me to choose different thoughts, envision what I desired and see the positive in the situations I had gone through. To this day, I appreciate those teachings, but it wasn't until I supplemented them with proper medical treatment that my mental health started to really improve.

After I graduated from PHP, one of my best friends told me I have a gift for glamorizing depression. She meant it as a compliment and I took it that way. Maybe I didn't need to study the Law of Attraction anymore. Maybe I had *become* it.

PART THREE
BEAUTY

SIXTEEN

UGLY MARKS

"Your imperfections are what make you beautiful."
—Sandra Bullock

You know those little marks on your skin that people call beauty marks? Why do they call them that? When everyone calls something beautiful that's actually *not* beautiful, it feels like everyone is lying. Why is *everyone* in on this lie?

I think that beauty marks should be called ugly marks.

Ever since I can remember, I've had marks on my arms, my back, my chest and my legs. On my left hand, I even have one on my pinkie finger, one on my middle finger and another on my thumb.

I've always thought my beauty marks were ugly marks. I didn't like having tiny spots all over my skin. I didn't want them, but they just kept coming. Every summer, more and more would show up. And they weren't anything like freckles. Freckles were cute! My dermatologist was never happy about them, either. See? It's not just me being superficial.

Maybe it's sweet that people call these blemishes beauty marks, but as soon as I can figure out how to get rid of mine in a healthy way, I will. That's how I approach beauty *and* life. If I don't like something, I change it or I change how I think about it. I live in a world of possibility.

A few years ago, I got dumped. At first, my pea brain tried to make it about my looks. *I'm not pretty enough!* Until then, it hadn't occurred to me that someone could break up with me because we weren't right for each other or that being rejected meant I was actually being saved from a relationship that wasn't worthy of me. I had always assumed it was about how I looked.

It was time to get over my old narrative. Plus, at the risk of sounding totally surface, the guy who broke up with me was *maybe* a four. I'm not just talking about looks here. I mean emotionally, spiritually and everything else.

You know when you look in the rearview at certain past relationships and scream, "What was I thinking?"

This was one of those situations.

Mid-breakup, a friend said, "This will be whatever you want it to be. If you want it to be sad and dramatic, it will be. But if you want to be empowered by it and turn it into a book or a business, you're capable of that, too."

My friend was right. There was always beauty in the breakdown. I just had to put on some waterproof mascara and dig for it. I had to turn what seemed like an ugly mark into something beautiful. I decided to feel my feelings until things felt pretty again. For two days, I cried myself to sleep. After that, it passed. Allowing things to get ugly opened up space for me to accept what had happened and move forward. Leaning into the ugliness somehow made everything pretty again.

Getting dumped always hurts. No one likes to have

their toys taken away before they're done playing with them, especially not me. It doesn't matter what type of training you've had, how spiritual you are or how much personal development work you've done. You still feel the pain, and you have to.

There's beauty in every breakdown because it's rich with honesty and vulnerability.

Every time you love, you get vulnerable. You let someone else *see* you, which includes the pretty parts *and* the parts that don't feel so pretty. For a species that so craves to be seen, we sure get twisted up when it actually happens.

Every time you love and get hurt, it's like dying. Whenever you choose to, whenever you feel strong enough, you can be reborn. If you love yourself, it doesn't matter who breaks up with you or how many ugly marks you have. You always get to start anew.

It works that way with beauty, too.

I've had many beauty rebirths, from Accutane and spray tanning to blowouts and fake nails. I've found that when you have a broken heart, beauty upgrades can help move the rebirth process along. Figuring out how to look good when you feel bad can go a long way. It might surprise you, but the most painful beauty rebirth I've experienced wasn't my nose job or any of my three tattoos. Nope. The most painful rebirth was microblading.

I'm not sure if you believe in reincarnation, but the whole idea is that you die and come back a better version of yourself. I've often wondered if you come back as a prettier version, too. Either way, I'm convinced microblading is beauty reincarnation—painful but so worth it.

I'VE BEEN WEARING makeup since middle school, but I always envied those girls who could go makeup-free. Did a potential reality exist where I didn't have to wear makeup, but still felt more confident than ever? I had bad acne for a long time. My middle school boyfriend called me "pizza face" when we broke up. I lusted over flawless skin—and I definitely didn't want to get teased—so in college, I asked my dermatologist about Accutane. After years of picking at my skin, I had bumps and scars. Since I was always obsessing over it, my skin had never really healed. After a short dose of Accutane, the acne and the scars went away. My skin isn't flawless, but I really don't *have* to wear makeup anymore. See, I manifested the impossible.

Still, I *do* wear makeup most days. It helps me feel more awake and ready for the day. But I don't *have* to wear it, and that's a big difference from how it was before. I'm more confident now.

How did I get to makeup-free me? In addition to medication, my dairy-free, sugar-free, gluten-free eating habits certainly help. My skin-care routine helps when I remember to do all the steps. But it's really microblading that sealed the deal.

The first time I got my eyebrows microbladed was right before my 30th birthday, right before I became Lyme-free. I was gearing up for a total reinvention. It was an expensive procedure, but I was running a profitable business, so I felt comfortable investing in my outer beauty, too. I'd only heard great things about microblading. If anyone had told me the truth-truth, that the pain of this procedure would push me to the edge of dying and coming back to life again, I might have continued to pencil in my brows forever. But here's the thing—the excruciating pain is worth it.

Here's how microblading works. The technician cuts

tiny hair-like lines into your brows with a mini razorblade, drips in a bit of dye and then lets it scab over. It's nasty, but it looks *so* good when it's done. In a way, you *are* letting your old eyebrows die so a new set can materialize in their place. A beauty rebirth!

I had a complicated relationship with my physical beauty until I had the revelation that beauty had something to teach me. I'm guessing you can relate. On the one hand, we want to be seen fully. On the other hand, we know calling attention to ourselves can open us up to critique.

Beauty *does* pave the way to being seen. When you show your beauty, you create the space to be acknowledged. You attract looks, comments and compliments. This type of attention is why some people avoid investing in their beauty. They don't want the comments or the compliments, and I get that.

As a child, I felt beautiful and I loved being seen. As a preteen, I couldn't have felt more awkward, and I wanted to hide. Throughout high school, college and my early adult years, I started to find my stride, develop my own look and see my beauty. But I won't lie. It took buckets of tears, tubes of mascara and a few beauty rebirths to get there.

Today, I'm comfortable being acknowledged for how I look as long as people also recognize my intelligence, my heart, my humor and my creativity. When I think back to how I was raised, that's the message I got as a child. My parents wanted me and my brothers to look good and *be* good, too.

As I got older, my self-image improved. I became more willing to be seen as I slowly made friends with my body, my face and my hair. If I wanted to be seen by others, I had to see myself first. A-line dresses? Not with this booty. Hair straightener? A necessity, until I sat my butt in a Drybar chair for the first time. Eyeliner? My eyes don't exist without it.

Beauty can help you heal. When you're sick or heart-broken, makeup helps. Spray tans help. Pretty clothes help. Beautiful things make us happy and investing in your beauty in an intentional way is well worth it.

A beautiful exterior isn't enough, though. Pain isn't pretty when it's just sitting there, eating away at you, even in your gorgeous packaging. If you let it, the pain will find its way into the cracks of your forehead and the frown lines on your face. Don't let pain sit inside of you. Let it wash over you instead.

You and I can debate beauty marks and ugly marks forever, but maybe there's something in the middle. Maybe they're just marks, like feelings are just feelings. Feelings don't have to be good or bad. They can just be. And it doesn't do any good for us to judge them.

SEVENTEEN

A WHOLE GLOW NEW WORLD

"Dreams are lovely. But they are just dreams. Fleeting, ephemeral, pretty. But dreams do not come true just because you dream them. It's hard work that makes things happen. It's hard work that creates change."

—Shonda Rhimes

When I graduated from Vanderbilt, I convinced my parents to let me move to New York City by getting a part-time internship in public relations at a fashion company and a second job as an executive assistant to the CEO of a boutique consulting firm. Both teams were small and fairly understaffed, so the pressure was on me to relieve the daily stress. One day, my boss gave my name to her friend, a *New York Times* bestselling author, and that led to a third gig ghostwriting articles for *Fast Company* and *HuffPost*.

At the fashion company, one of our celebrity clients was Jenny Humphrey from *Gossip Girl*. I watched *Gossip Girl* religiously, but I didn't understand why everyone was so stressed about her coming into the office. It wasn't like she was the *least* important person in the show, but it wasn't like she was *Serena van der Woodsen* or, God forbid, *Blair Waldorf*. One day, my boss scolded me for putting the hangers in the wrong direction, and later vented to me over lunch about how the job was so below her. She was meant to be working at Chanel, or so she thought.

The best thing I learned from this internship was that I didn't want any of it for the long-term. I'd watched *The Devil Wears Prada* enough times to know working in fashion would be anything but glamorous, but when I realized I didn't even like the clothes—or the people—my time was up. I no longer wanted to work in an environment where I wasn't learning, enjoying myself or contributing to the world in some meaningful way. Chasing glitter was leaving me feeling empty.

When I left the fashion company, I went full-time at the consulting firm, where I was learning every single day. I learned about digital marketing, the ins and outs of running a startup and how to network my ass off. Most importantly, I learned to fake it until I made it.

Our CEO hooked me up with some incredible experiences. She was a powerful woman in her mid-30s going after her goals in the City of Dreams. I joined just as she was starting the company and she taught me a lot about the early startup days of a business. She also exposed me to New York on a deeper level. She introduced me to the Step Up Women's Network and helped me snag a spot as the youngest person on their junior board of directors. It was through that organization that I met Gabby Bernstein in 2010—a game-changing experience for me. Thanks to Step Up, I got involved with another women's group called 85 Broads, through which I met the serial entrepreneur and media mogul Gary Vaynerchuk. Our CEO sent me on the writing retreat where I met feminist author Erica Jong, the one who urged me to start writing in the first place.

One day, she sat me down and told me that although all our clients loved me, I didn't have any "hard skills." Business was growing, and although I was smart and fast, eventually I didn't have the skillset our CEO needed. She became hypercritical—not only of how I worked, but also of how I dressed. She wasn't happy with me, but she also didn't know how to let me go. When she said she wasn't pleased with my presentation in front of our biggest client and suggested I should have stayed at the office even later (when I had been there until 2 am), I knew my time was up.

I got a job at another startup, selling search engine optimization and pay-per-click ads to small business owners. I fell in love with the fast-paced energy and the competitive sales environment. I was inspired, learned quickly and did well, seeing my name on leaderboards and winning a competition to spend a day in the CEO's office just months after my start. There were sales trips, holiday parties and company-wide rallies. It felt like a family. I made a whole crew of new best friends. I also met and fell in love with a guy named PJ. His best friend was my assigned mentor, but PJ had his own agenda and started coaching and training me in sales. Between the strong culture and commitment to mentorship, the job taught me how to believe in myself again.

Working in sales gave me a new skillset and helped me regain my confidence, but my days lacked depth and meaning. At work, I cold-called plastic surgeons and med spas and sold them online advertising. At home, I read and wrote in my journal. On weekends, I partied through my frustrations. Was this all my life would ever be?

"I CAN'T DO THIS ANYMORE," I told my dad one day as I called him crying from the office bathroom, praying that none of my co-workers would open the door. "All I do is make phone calls all day. Is this it? Is this all my life is going to be?"

"If you find a job you love, it won't feel like work," Dad said. "You know this."

I did know.

"Your dream job might not exist yet. You might have to create it. In the meantime, think about coming home for a little while."

It didn't matter how many times I jumped from one job to the next. My life was a broken record of jobs that didn't quite fit, and I was the one letting it stay that way. All the things I was afraid of wasting—time, money and energy—I was wasting anyway by being so unhappy.

I thought I would find myself in New York City, but I soon realized I could only find myself within me.

Still unsure of my purpose but determined to figure it out, I left New York and moved back home to D.C. With the support of family and the familiarity of home, I hoped I'd know what steps to take next.

I knew I needed to be working on my own and I had so many ideas for blogs, businesses and books, but I had no clue where to start. Eventually, I narrowed it down to two (still very broad) options: go back to school or start my own business.

To maximize my options, I submitted grad school

applications for a master's degree in nutrition while brainstorming side hustle ideas for a business.

One day while scrolling through social media, I saw a meme that said, "If she can do it, so can you." For whatever reason, Amy flashed into my mind.

AMY WAS the woman who did my spray tans when I lived in New York City. I found her online, because her spray tan business happened to be the closest one to my apartment. After my first appointment, I quickly became addicted to her $50, 15-minute service. Every two weeks, I'd walk my sun-deprived self over to her fancy Gramercy Park apartment and sneak past the doorman.

Amy was a perfectly bronzed billboard for her own business and her apartment smelled like a manufactured but enticing blend of fake coconuts and fake tan. As she sprayed me, I'd catch a glance at a photo of Amy and her hot fiancé. As I was in life purpose search mode myself, I started to ask myself questions about her life. *Is she happy spray tanning naked people all day? Is this what I need to do to get a hot husband, have a hot bod and finally be happy?*

When I saw this meme—"If she can do it, so can you"— I was immediately transported back to Amy's apartment and the feeling of being there. I loved beauty. I felt noticeably better about myself when I was tan. I believed in the product and the service. If Amy could do it, couldn't I do it, too?

I wanted to reach out to Amy, who was gorgeous, successful and very busy, but I wasn't sure if it was the right thing to do. She was running her own business, and I was worried she wouldn't have time for me. I asked for a sign from the universe.

As I was wondering if I should email her, she reached out to me. "Now that February is coming to a close and spring is right around the corner, it's the perfect time to start prepping your bikini bod," she wrote. "What better way to get motivated than with a gorgeous glow!!"

Clearly it was a mass email, but the timing was specific enough for me. I took it as the sign I needed. I wrote a response, letting her know I had moved to D.C. and wanted to set up my own mobile spray tanning business. I asked if she had any advice on where to start.

Amy responded the next day to let me know she was slammed with clients but would get back to me over the weekend. I was relieved. Getting a response—even if it was only promising a real one later—felt like a nudge from the universe.

Amy followed up with me that weekend. She told me buying the machine would be my first step, but that developing a marketing strategy and establishing a clientele would be the hard part. She explained it took her almost two years to get up and running with graphic design, websites and search engine optimization. Since most of my work experience was in marketing, public relations and sales, I hoped I'd have a shorter start-up time.

Meanwhile, a salesperson from the manufacturer had responded to my inquiry. We discussed my options, and I pulled together $3,000 from my personal savings to make my very first investment in my very first business, a mobile spray tanning machine and lots of fake tanning solution.

I kept my expectations realistic. I wasn't trying to build a million-dollar spray tan business overnight. I wanted to open the door to working for myself and kick-start my journey toward the freedom I was craving.

There I was, 24 years old and starting my first official business—airbrush spray tanning. I set up my studio in the living room of my one-bedroom apartment. After meditating and throwing ideas at my boyfriend for hours, I landed on the name: Whole Glow.

If you haven't had an airbrush tan, you should know it's an intimate experience. You strip down to your panties (or nothing at all), step into the tan tent and a skilled technician sprays your entire body, cracks and crevices included. When the tan is fully developed a few hours later, you're glowing from head to toe—and calculating how to afford the habit regularly, even if it means getting naked in front of a stranger on a weekly basis.

But getting naked wasn't the only way to be vulnerable at Whole Glow. It turned out there was a much deeper layer.

"HOW'S IT GOING?"

Without much more prompting than a simple hello, clients would spill the most intimate details of their lives. The tan tent became a confessional of sorts. I was the therapist and my clients were the patients, but instead of lying on a couch, clients were standing butt naked in my tan tent and baring their souls. You've probably heard people say that hairstylists have heard all the secrets in the world. Spray tan artists have heard even more.

I loved having my own business, I loved making money and I loved making people feel good in their bodies. Most of all, I loved people sharing their secrets with me. Sometimes my clients opened up so much that they cried, forcing me to dab their tears to prevent any streaks. Appointments were 20 minutes each, but my clients managed to squeeze in full-on therapy sessions. We talked about dead-end relationships, lost jobs, cheating husbands, mom guilt and loved ones who'd passed to the other side. There were the celebratory moments, too: nearly-published books, a second date after a dry spell, promotions at work, engagements and, of course, weddings.

There were so many weddings.

Brides were the worst. They always had to come in twice—and sometimes more—just to test the color. I required it, but that didn't mean I liked it. It was a protective measure in a terrifying territory. The last thing you want is a bride calling the day before her wedding saying she looks orange and begging you to drag your spray tan equipment to her mother's house to fix it (been there).

Brides also asked the same repetitive questions, all of which had obvious and highly disappointing answers. Was it possible for the spray tan to rub off on their *very, very, very* expensive dresses? I wanted to ask if they'd ever gotten a spray tan and then slept on crisp white sheets. If you sweat one drop, you're screwed.

Brides were typically a little bit rude. Most of the time, I couldn't blame them. They were stressed to the max and often accompanied by their mother (or mother-in-law-to-be), which only added to the pressure.

The worst part about spray tanning brides, though, was that they all said the same dreadful thing: "I'm just ready for the wedding to be over." This came as a shock to me. Marriage seemed like the ultimate goal. I couldn't bear the idea that women were spending decades dreaming of "the one," but when it came down to the actual wedding day, they couldn't wait for it to be over.

In the tan tent confessional, I learned that at the exact moment when society says women are supposed to feel their happiest and *most* beautiful, most aren't feeling good at all. I was getting a glimpse of the truth-truth.

I was intrigued by the outpouring of honesty I heard in the tan tent, but I was also unprepared. Did I have the proper training to be counseling my clients? Um, probably not.

When I launched Whole Glow, I thought I was getting into the beauty industry, but without meaning to, I seemed to have entered the realm of mental health. My new role as a sort-of-therapist had me questioning myself. I was excited, a bit weirded out and very curious. My heart was cracked open. I had reverence for every story I heard and every tear I quickly wiped away (no streaking!). My clients were coming in for their outer glow, but they were leaving with an inner glow, too.

I wondered if, on some spiritual level, I was meant to be meeting these women and impacting their lives in this intimate way. They came in under the guise of wanting a tan before a vacation, but as we peeled back the layers, what they really wanted was to understand why they'd created lives they needed to take a vacation from in the first place. They came in saying they wanted to feel sexy when they saw their ex-lover over the weekend, but what they really wanted was to know if they'd ever find love again. Each tan began to feel like a divine exchange. The outer glow was the access point to the inner glow and I was there to witness their transformation.

There was one thing that stood in the way of almost every transformation: self-loathing, and a lot of it. Women had a knack for hating on themselves, especially when it came time to get naked. I remembered feeling vulnerable and insecure when I'd been in Amy's tan tent so I understood the feeling. It took me a minute, however, to understand how to respond in the most effective way.

I had a few options. The first was to totally disagree with them.

Client: "Ugh, you're going to see my stretch marks."

Me: "What are you talking about?! I don't see a stretch mark in sight!"

This approach rarely worked. People—especially naked ones—can tell when you're lying. Lying breaks trust, trust is the number one ingredient in any sale and sales are required to run a business. I had to find a way to be at least semi-honest.

The second option was to change the subject.

Client: "I forgot to shave my legs and missed my last wax appointment. I'm a mess."

Me: "Um, can you believe how gorgeous it is outside today?"

This strategy didn't work, either. It felt abrupt and rude. My only remaining option was to make a rule. "No self-deprecation in the tan tent!" I said this on the fly to a client who was hating on her literally-just-had-a-baby bod and it stuck.

The rule allowed me to change the dynamic of our tan tent confessionals. Clients could share their stories, but there was no room for self-hate. It was a fast and light way to show that even spray tanning was an act of self-love. No shit talking allowed. Clients loved it, remembered it and started saying it back to me.

I LIKE to say that beauty was one of my first and most meaningful teachers. My clients taught me a lot—and very quickly. Beauty is more about seeing yourself than it is about vanity. I had clients with skin diseases who wanted to even out their skin tone and clients who wanted to cover their head-to-toe scars from years of drug use. One repeat client had been injured in a car bomb attack in Iraq. Spray tanning wasn't just for pasty white girls, either. In fact, it wasn't just for women at all. The tan tent needed to be a safe and self-loving space across the board. People came to me to get tan, but also to feel confident and comfortable in their own skin. Sometimes, they wanted their old skin back. Sometimes, they wanted to feel brand new. My intention was never to change anyone, but to add a little boost so they could glow through whatever they were going through.

Through the experience of spraying and listening, I learned that how women feel about their external beauty is deeply connected to how they feel about themselves. For my clients, their outer appearance was an entry point into their Greatest Level of Want—or, as I like to call it, their G.L.O.W. Ultimately, what they wanted wasn't a spray tan. It was a sense of peace.

The intimate conversations I had with clients in the tan tent would become the inspiration that opened me to the world of coaching. In the meantime, my tanning business grew—and much faster than I expected. I moved the operation out of my home and partnered with local gyms. I hired an assistant I adored.

I felt an urgency to support my clients now rather than wait two years to graduate from my nutrition program. Plus, I knew it wouldn't matter if they ate all the kale in the world if they didn't love themselves first. Having seen an obvious tie between inner and outer beauty that I couldn't ignore, I dropped out of the grad school program I had just started and began a training program to become a life coach. Coach training became the crash course I desperately needed. I brought the lessons I learned in class back to the spray tan confessional. The outer glow was the tanning and the inner glow was the coaching. Together, they made up a client's Whole Glow.

My clients left the tent looking flawless, but that didn't mean they were no longer in pain. Again and again, I held back the temptation to say, "At least you look good!" as my clients shared their complicated life stories. If anyone knew looking good didn't necessarily mean feeling good, it was me.

Looking at how my career has evolved, I see how beauty became an access point to a much larger conversation.

Not every woman is ready to hire a life coach, and for many, it's too "out there." They'll stick with therapy or happy hour with the girls. I know part of my purpose is to broaden the connection between inner and outer beauty and make working on yourself as mainstream as investing in Kylie Jenner's next lip kit. There are no easy fixes in beauty or life, but investing in beauty services that make you feel good is a start. Get the spray tan. Plump your lips. Try the expensive moisturizer. Buy the dress. Working on your outer beauty won't "fix" your inner problems, but it might help you gain the confidence to take bigger, bolder steps in the direction of your dreams. It always has for me.

EIGHTEEN

THE KIM KARDASHIAN OF SELF-HELP

"I'm an entrepreneur. 'Ambitious' is my middle name."

—Kim Kardashian West

When I was a preteen, I had a vision of myself as a tanned, sexy, exotic-looking woman. But I felt pale, mousy and average-looking. I was frustrated that my fantasy and my reality weren't matching up. I knew it would feel good to finally look like the woman I felt like inside. It took decades, but brick by brick (and beauty treatment by beauty treatment), I started to align my vision with reality.

Manifestation is a complicated process, and it's not without its hiccups. Take my experience with bright red lipstick. A few years ago, bright red lipstick peaked in popularity. I was intrigued by it, but refused to wear it myself. I wasn't ready for the attention it would attract. It felt like something the sexier version of myself I'd dreamed of as a kid would wear.

I stared at pictures of women in magazines who were brave enough to wear red lipstick and wondered what it felt like to be them. I admired their ease with their beauty and their confidence in showing it off. I would glance at women I noticed at restaurants, the flickering candlelight high-lighting their juicy red lips and wonder if they wrote poetry in the mornings and traveled to Spain for long weekends. I figured that a woman wearing such distinct red lipstick also had to be happy and self-aware—aware, at the very least, of the impact of her beauty.

For me, wearing red lipstick meant being seen and acknowledged. And it was a declaration that I was *ready* to be seen. But "ready" isn't real. Nobody feels fully ready for the great debuts of their lives.

If I had the level of self-awareness then that I have now, I would have gone through my own manifestation process: *seeing* myself wearing the red lipstick and owning my beauty; *feeling* the experience of wearing the lipstick and being seen; *being* the confident, brave woman who knows her power and wears red lipstick. Then I would have *done* it! I would have worn the lipstick and let myself *have* those juicy red lips right then and there. I would have owned my power full force, "ready" or not.

But I wasn't that self-aware in my early entrepreneurial days. I was utilizing my full-time job as my "investor" in my real dreams and hustling to grow my spray tanning business on the side. I was playing with entrepreneurship, but I didn't have a master plan. I needed an extra push.

That push came in the form of a mentor and entrepreneur I admired, Nisha Moodley. Later, Nisha would become my coach, teacher and friend, but she started as my glamour. The word "glamour" originally referred to a magic spell, an illusion cast by witches. Witches used glamours to shift their appearances for disguise. But a glamour doesn't have to be used for hiding. It can give you a vision of who you want to become.

When you see what you desire for yourself in someone else, you feel a sense of magnetism. Jealousy isn't allowed, though. You have to be inspired by what you see in that other person without taking anything from them.

To me, Nisha was the embodiment of inner *and* outer beauty. She owned both of them, which was why I was so attracted to her work, her writings and her teachings. Nisha knew herself and that was something I wanted. Nisha also wore bright red lipstick.

ON THE SPECIAL day I worked up the courage to wear red lipstick for the first time, do you know where I went?

The gym.

One of my Whole Glow locations was at this gym, so I wasn't anonymous. Wearing red lipstick felt a little rebellious and totally unnecessary. Physically, I was going to exercise, but spiritually, I had a different agenda—owning my beauty.

On the way there, I felt nervous and excited. I wondered if anyone would ask me why I was wearing bright red lipstick to work out. I walked in, greeted the staff and smiled at a few friends. I made eye contact with a cute guy I'd never seen and he gave me a look that meant he noticed me.

Even though looking back at this scene makes me laugh, it was a turning point for me. I don't think anyone noticed my red lipstick specifically, but they did notice *me*. It had never been about the lipstick. It was about what happened *inside* when I put it on. With a swipe of red lipstick, I became my next-level me.

I still wear lipstick. My favorite shade these days is a light pink lip stain by Yves Saint Laurent, but I did pull out a bright red hue for a recent photo shoot and was reminded of how red elevates my energy. Whether it's red, pink or something much bolder, if it says, "Look at me," then you're owning the brightness of your beauty.

Some days, I'm really glammed up. Other days, I don't get out of my pajamas or wear any makeup at all. But I do pop on my pink lip stain when I go live on social media or FaceTime with a friend, because it helps me feel more confident. It helps me feel more like myself. It's the third step in my manifesting process. With a bold lip on, I'm *being* the woman I always wanted to be. It makes me feel more like me.

Find your own glamours and use them to help manifest your future you. Your outer beauty is only as valuable as the inner beauty that goes with it, though. So, if you're investing in blowouts but not books, we need to talk.

Beauty is a form of self-expression. It's also a form of gratitude. It's how we honor ourselves and open up to others. Own your beauty. Express it, enhance it and be willing to spend money on it. Beauty is an art and an experiment. It allows you to experience yourself. That's why true physical beauty is less about conventional standards and more about self-expression.

Express your inner beauty by sharing your feelings, writing your truth, collaborating with others, telling your story, being vulnerable and serving your community.

Express your outer beauty by getting a fresh haircut, dancing in your bedroom, wearing clothes that make you feel alive, trying a bolder lipstick and playing up your eyes.

You can *tell* if someone is using their beauty to express themselves or if they're using it to meet some sort of social standard. Either you're moving toward self-actualization or trying to desperately validate your self-worth.

For me, bright red lipstick was a way to access my next level of power. Eventually, I needed to move into new, uncharted territory, which meant another glamour.

———

"LOOK what Kim Kardashian did with that sex tape. You're going to be the Kim Kardashian of self-help!"

This was Susie's evidence for making her point: I needed to use my unfortunate diagnosis with Lyme disease as a force for creating good in my life.

"Lyme is just a storyline. Stop complaining about it and use it."

I met Susie in my coach training class in 2013. She'd always been a supportive friend and once she got over the idea that she "didn't have friends, only fans" as a stand-up comedian, I wiggled my way into her inner world and we became very close. Susie was the first friend who saw me fully. She was always saying how creative, smart and business savvy I was. I felt like she understood me inside and out. I had never felt so seen, heard or understood in a friendship.

While I was going through coach training, I was also wrestling with my identity. I had a few boyfriends during the year-long program, but nothing serious. Really, I was dating my girlfriends, especially Susie and Desi.

Susie talked about beauty a lot. She was constantly telling me and Desi to own our beauty. She made jokes onstage about how she felt about her looks, which seemed to me like the ultimate form of confidence. Susie was a genius at taking the hard parts of life and making something beautiful from them. At the very least, she could make them funny.

Although Susie was always joking, she was dead serious about some things. When she told me I was going to be the Kim Kardashian of self-help, I believed her. I also thought it was a good comparison. The Kardashians are geniuses at turning potential setbacks into success.

Kim owns her beauty, her voice, her power and her mistakes. She's a boss, a mogul, a mom and a wife. She's evolved from Paris Hilton's assistant with the sex tape to the Kim Kardashian West we know today, pursuing her law degree to help with prison reform. Borrowing from Kim at any stage of her evolution to help me navigate my own moments of rapid expansion has been seriously helpful. In my personal manifesting process, I sometimes ask myself: *What would Kim Kardashian do?*

It's glamour magic and manifesting rolled into one. I get to use present Kim to help create the Katie of the future.

What would Kim do if her assistant quit? Find a new one.

What would Kim do if her relationship ended? Find a new one.

What would Kim do if her Met Gala dress just wasn't working? Find a new one.

What would Kim do if she didn't like her nose? Find a new one.

One day, I asked myself that last question for real.

"IF YOU WANT to do it, I'll pay for it," Gram said.

We were shopping the racks at Bloomingdale's when I casually mentioned a nose job. I was 14, maybe 15.

For most of my childhood, people talked about my nose. It was one of the traits I got from my dad. And I really, really wanted to look like my mom.

"If Gram's offering and you really want it, take her up on it," Mom said. "She might not offer to pay for it later on!"

It would take over a decade to decide to get a nose job and I would be the one shelling out the cold, hard cash. Thanks to the 24-month, no-interest deal, I got to enjoy my appearance without breaking the bank. And I waited until I was old enough to make sure it was a change I really wanted to make. It's not a Google doc. There's no "undo" button for plastic surgery.

I may spend a lot of time doing inner work, but that doesn't mean I'm above seeking expert help when I want outer transformation. Plastic surgery can be a divisive topic, but I'd always wanted to get my nose tweaked. When I sat down for my first rhinoplasty consultation at 28 and the surgeon asked how long I'd wanted to get the procedure done, I said, "Forever."

Of course, the person who loved my new nose the most was my Gram. Unexpectedly, the person who was most upset by my new nose was Susie.

When I'd told Susie my plans, she said I was already so pretty and that if I had to fix my nose, she couldn't be friends with me anymore. I thought she was joking, since she was *always* joking, but as our friendship started to fade, it became clear that she was serious this time too.

Beauty is deeply personal. I've learned that what I want for myself is not always the same as what others want for me. But I didn't understand how Susie saying I was Kim

Kardashian Jr. lined up with her hating the idea of a nose job.

Of course, you don't *need* a nose job, a spray tan or even a blowout to achieve success, but if those things make you feel more like yourself, then why not?

I get that celebrities like the Kardashians have played a serious role in supporting our unhealthy obsession with appearances. Hollywood gives us an unreasonable standard of beauty to live up to. I'm constantly torn as to whether changing myself is a feminist expression of freedom or evidence of my own unrelenting obsession with impossible beauty standards.

At its core, beauty is about letting yourself be seen. I've learned that sometimes people hide their beauty because they're afraid they have too much. They don't want to show off, so they don't show anything at all. People may also hide their beauty because they're afraid they have too little. They don't want to feel insecure, less than or invisible, so they just go invisible on their own.

I encourage you to do whatever you need to do to be seen. As you invest in your beauty, you need to understand one thing: You are already perfect. You are already whole and nothing external will make you feel complete. Like the smell of fresh leather in a brand-new car wears off after a while, so does the newness of any beauty enhancement. You will be left with the same you, so you must learn to love that you.

Before you can love yourself, you have to see yourself. It doesn't matter how beautiful you are if your eyes are closed. What got me to finally open mine? Seeing all those naked bodies and makeup-free faces in my spray tan tent. Once I saw the truth-truth—that most people have cellulite *and* a morning face—I could see myself with clearer eyes.

Much of the comparison game happens with celebrities, social media influencers and models in magazines. But a lot of the most harmful comparisons happen when you put yourself up against your best friends, your colleagues, your family members and the random girl walking down the street who you swear your partner checked out.

Like you, I always knew celebrities were being airbrushed and otherwise falsely represented. But even "normal" people don't show their natural selves. Since there was no filter in the tan tent, I saw acne scars, stretch marks, cankles and nipple hair that poked out so far it almost hit me in the face. When I put myself in the middle of this wide range of women, I saw that I was actually pretty average. I realized I was enough. I got to stop comparing myself to the fully made-up versions of women I saw walking down the street, because I got real about the secret efforts it took to get there. The "natural look" often requires Spanx, four-inch heels, a push-up bra, contouring *and* a professional blowout.

The path to real beauty starts with a simple intention. Maybe you say, *I want to feel beautiful. I want to feel at peace with who I am today and who I am becoming. I want to really love myself.*

What are you doing with your beauty right now? The outside can reflect the inside, but the inside is the priority. At the core, it's all inner work, because it doesn't matter if everyone in the world sees your beauty, your essence and your power. If *you* don't see it, you won't be able to accept the acknowledgment of others. We often think we want the acceptance of a lover or friend, but what we really desire is love and validation from ourselves.

We want to see ourselves and to be ourselves.

NINETEEN
THUNDER THIGHS

"I have insecurities of course, but I don't hang out with anyone who points them out to me."
—Adele

Even for the future Kim Kardashian of self-help, middle school was tough. If you ask me why I didn't think I was pretty until much later, it's simple: I really wasn't, at least not in the traditional sense. Until I was about 10 years old, I looked like one of those perfect American Girl dolls in my closet, free of ugly marks, acne or anything of the sort. Then the teen years hit me hard. I wasn't emotionally prepared for the impact they would have on my self-image. I was chubby with braces, bangs and baggy jeans. I still had this future vision of myself as a conventionally beautiful woman, but I looked awkward and felt that way, too.

My best friend called me "thunder thighs." Another friend said I was the queen of the itty-bitty titty committee. A girl I barely knew spread a rumor that I stuffed my butt (not my bra, *my butt*). I started to lose confidence and doubt myself.

Beyond making fun of my body, my best friend—clearly, less of a best friend and more of a bully—said she was the pretty one and I was the smart one. I didn't like the thought that I would never get to experience liking how I looked, but it was more important to me not to be dumb, so I leaned in to being smart. What choice did I have? I was certain that I'd eventually get my *She's All That* moment and the cute guy, too.

I felt better about myself in high school. As a freshman with a sophomore boyfriend, I got a jump-start in the confidence department. As a sophomore, I ran for vice president of the student government and won. My crush—who would soon become my next long-term boyfriend—was a lacrosse and football player who endorsed me to the entire student body. My junior year, I was elected president. My senior year, we were voted "class couple" and I won homecoming queen.

My relationship with my physical appearance continued evolving as I got older. I started to accept myself. I learned how to style my hair. Highlights and hair straighteners were early miracles that showed me I could make small external changes and experience major internal shifts. I was starting to like how I looked! I felt confident. For the first time, there seemed to be room for the smart girl *and* the sexy girl to exist in one body.

The summer after senior year was also the summer of the tick bite that changed the course of my life. The amazing feeling of both looking good on the outside and feeling good on the inside—which I was just starting to hack —was short-lived.

But for nearly a decade after high school, I didn't *know* I had Lyme, which made my experience with beauty a stressful one in college and beyond. According to the *Princeton Review*, Vandy had the happiest students *and* the most beautiful campus. A popular dating site said it was second only to Yale in terms of student body hotness. My classmates were well-dressed, well-spoken and well-off. Greek life was important and the fraternity and sorority houses were home base for non-stop drinking and partying. There were at least 20 parties happening on any given weekend.

Really, it was the most stressful school I could have gone to. I was expected to be the perfect student *and* the perfect party girl. It was a lot of pressure and it was difficult to manage as I started the long journey of battling and diagnosing a chronic illness.

Trying to find my flow with beauty in college, I experimented with my style. My preppy look got a trendy edge when I broke up with my high school boyfriend who I'd been dating long distance while he played lacrosse at Bucknell. It was meant to be a temporary break while I studied abroad in Australia, a choice I made because I was craving adventure, but as soon as I got there, I felt different. Something was shifting inside of me. I was drawing inspiration and influence from my new surroundings.

There was so much *natural* beauty in Australia. My best friend, Lindsay, and I lived on Dolphin Street in Coogee Beach, a coastal suburb of Sydney. Every day, the broad, sandy beach would fill with swimmers, surfers, families and study abroad kids like us. It was almost impossible to get motivated to go to class when we lived one block from the beach and were still hungover from a night of dancing at the fancy clubs downtown. But Sydney was so ripe for exploration that we never wanted to stay in bed, no matter how intense our hangovers were. We'd sleep with our windows open, wake up to the birds chirping and do our morning run along the coastline to Bondi Beach.

Australia gave me a chance to experiment. What was beautiful there was very different from what was beautiful in our hometown of Annapolis. Back home, beauty was a Lilly Pulitzer dress, boat shoes and straight blonde hair. At Vanderbilt, it was black leggings, stacks of David Yurman bracelets and a Louis Vuitton tote. Beauty in Australia was bright makeup, naturally curly hair, skin-tight dresses and neon crop tops.

My conception of what was beautiful changed when I lived in Australia, and the concept of beauty as a changeable thing fascinated me. My ideas about beauty were evolving as I was evolving. And very importantly, I was realizing that the way I presented myself to the world had the ability to shift my experience.

———

"NO MORE CRYING IN PUBLIC," my mom said.

I was crying my way through a Sunday shopping trip to Bloomingdale's.

After my brother died, all the pain that had been buried under my anxiety was finally released. In order to make up for feeling so emotionally repressed for most of my life, I spent two years crying through every family outing, whether it was a shopping day with my mom or a fancy dinner with my parents, grandparents and my other brother, Johnny. I didn't care about how I looked anymore. All I wanted was to *feel*.

My mom was shockingly cool about my new flirtation with emotions—until she wasn't. She was probably right to shut me down because my crying in public was getting out of hand. I started to rein it in by stopping the tears as soon as I felt them coming on. It turns out that people on reality TV tap the inner corners of their eyes for a few reasons. It prevents them from crying—and, of course, from smearing their makeup.

At first, I was afraid that if I didn't let the tears flow out whenever I felt them coming, they'd get stuck somewhere deep within me and lodge there, maybe forever. But that's not true. With time, I've gotten better at understanding and sharing my feelings. More often than not, I don't need the tears to speak for me anymore.

I grew up highly aware of how I looked and much less aware of how I felt. It wasn't until I was in training to become a life coach that I even started gaining awareness around my own feelings. When our trainers asked us to identify our feelings, needs and desires, I drew a blank. I realized I hadn't ever thought much about how I felt. *How do I feel? Happy? Sad? Excited? Embarrassed? Frustrated? Grateful? Angry? Anxious? Hopeful? Bored as hell?* Often, it was a unique cocktail.

Why was I so unfamiliar with my own feelings for so long? I think one reason is that all my emotions were overtaken by a single overpowering state: anxiety.

THE ONGOING MISSION TO understand feelings is one reason Liv and I are so compatible. The other day, she called me frustrated with a dating situation. She was repeating a pattern she wanted to break, but as hard as she tried, she kept attracting the same situation, even with different men.

"Listen, Liv," I said. "I know you *think* you don't like the dynamic, but if it's still going on, there's a part of you that does."

"Say more," she said.

"We get comfortable with feelings we've experienced in the past, even if we've evolved beyond them. Even if we consciously don't want to repeat those dynamics, they're familiar, and we like familiar. We keep repeating the same patterns, even when we say we don't want to, because we're used to them. We keep recreating what we're used to until we do the deeper work to change it."

"That makes sense," she said.

"What feeling do you keep experiencing?" I asked.

"That's what I can't figure out. I just left therapy. My therapist asked how I felt about Derrick and I told her I felt deceived, but she said deceived isn't a feeling. As I was leaving, she handed me a list of feelings."

There we were, in our early 30s, still learning what feelings were and walking around with lists of them in our Saint Laurent bags. We were running a company that teaches women how to use their feelings to guide them to their true desires, dreams and goals. Meanwhile, we were still trying to figure out what a feeling was to begin with. The old adage is true: You really do teach what you need to learn.

Here's what I've learned: Your subconscious memories are so strong that you will continue to relate to yourself as who you were in childhood until you do the work to reprogram old thought patterns and beliefs.

For example, if hearing my middle school best friend call me "thunder thighs" made me feel bad about my body, I'll continue to feel bad whenever I notice my thighs *unless* I reprogram the story. If I switch it up and tell myself I love my thick, juicy thighs, my middle school best friend's voice gets quieter and mine gets louder.

For the record, this is why I love Beyoncé. Not only does she turn lemons into lemonade, she's played a huge role in shifting our collective narrative about how hot curves can be. Every time I see her signature so-called thunder thighs on a magazine cover, it helps reinforce my new beliefs about my thickness. The more evidence you find to support the reprogramming, the faster it'll happen.

Here are some of the other old stories about beauty that I've had to rewrite:

If my skin breaks out, even my boyfriend will tease me.
My boobs are so small that even my friends will make fun of them.
My butt is so big that it looks fake.

These stories weren't true. They were isolated incidents that became very loud.

Before I even knew I could reprogram these thoughts, I learned how to hide my face with makeup. I learned how to cover up my thighs and wear padded bras to make my boobs look bigger. I learned how to explain away my body. Every time someone looked at me, I assumed they were judging me. *Don't worry, my skin will clear up soon! I just ran three miles because I'm working on my legs! I'll wear a push-up bra! I swear my butt is real!*

It took a long time to heal and recognize my true beauty. All the friends, boyfriends and total strangers who have loved and complimented the real me couldn't fix the hurt that had been caused in middle school. The key was doing the work *myself*.

TWENTY

THE BEAUTY DISCONNECT

"I have my flaws, but I embrace them and I love them because they're mine."
—Winnie Harlow

"I can't wear sleeveless shirts," my mom said as she turned from side to side, reviewing her profile in the dressing room.

I asked her why not.

"My arms are too skinny." Mom seemed frustrated and upset with her body. I looked in the mirror, tugged my shirt down over my little tummy and felt frustrated and upset with my body, too.

My mom is very beautiful. At the grocery store, people stop, swear they know her from somewhere and then tell her she looks like Sally Field, only prettier. As a kid, all I wanted was to look like her. But I didn't. I looked like my dad. People would say, "You've got your dad's brown eyes!" "You've got your dad's big smile!" "You've got your dad's Italian nose!"

As I grew older, I realized I also had my dad's arms and my dad's legs, because I surely didn't have my mom's. There was nothing about me that was too skinny. Having grown up with a constant awareness that I had a mom who belonged in Hollywood, it didn't feel good to only be compared to my father, despite the fact that he would have fit in in Hollywood, too. It didn't matter how good-looking my father was—I didn't want to look like a handsome man. I wanted to be *beautiful*.

As I got older and settled more fully into my own skin, something interesting started to happen. Almost every time I was out with my mom, people would ask if we were sisters. We'd just giggle and play along. Finally, it clicked. If my mom was as beautiful as everyone always said she was and I looked like her sister, then I must be beautiful, too. I felt a sense of relief.

MANY PEOPLE FEEL a disconnect between how they look on the outside and how they feel on the inside. They look at themselves and don't see the person they are on the inside—or they can't bear to look at themselves at all. Haven't you heard about those people who avoid mirrors?

It's taken me decades, thousands of dollars in therapy and more beauty treatments than I can count to start to connect my inner and outer selves. My goal is to make sure what I feel on the inside is being reflected on the outside and vice versa. But just because I'm willing to look in the mirror doesn't mean I always love what I see. The difference as an adult is that if I don't like it, I know I can change it.

Sometimes you feel the connection between your inner

and outer beauty and sometimes you don't. Maybe you wake up after a restful night, look in the mirror and think, *Wow, my morning face is actually quite sexy.*

Maybe you get a blowout and put on a dress that hugs all the right places. Suddenly, you feel more like yourself than ever before. It lasts through the evening (or the next morning, if you're lucky) and then you wake up groggy, can barely button your skinny jeans and pick a ridiculous fight with your partner because you've convinced yourself they don't think you're pretty anymore. In reality, *you* don't think you're pretty, even though only 10 hours before you thought you were a total babe. Beauty is a complete mind game.

"HI, it's nice to meet you," I said as I tentatively shook hands. "I'm Katie De..."

This was how I used to introduce myself to people. The last part was slurred and almost inaudible. I couldn't even say my own name with confidence.

One day, I noticed my meek introduction at a networking event and knew I needed to do some work, so I went to the mirror. If I wanted the world to see me, I needed to practice seeing myself first.

I sat on the floor in front of my mirror and imagined myself speaking on one of the world's largest stages. Practice builds confidence. I now prep for speeches, podcasts, classes and meetings in front of the mirror.

When you try it, start by introducing yourself to yourself. Even if it's uncomfortable (it's meant to be!), talk to yourself out loud. Notice your facial expressions, your tone of voice and how you feel. Then, acknowledge yourself. Tell yourself how great you're doing, how proud you are of you.

Then, practice what you need to practice, whether it's a difficult conversation with a team member, a public speaking engagement, a heartfelt apology or a vulnerable admission of your personal truth.

You know the rules. If you want to be loved, admired, respected and even revered, you have to do it for yourself first. Mirror work is about loving yourself, knowing yourself and seeing yourself. It's a way to be your own mentor, teacher and guide.

When you love yourself in every direction—from the inside out and the outside in—you are loved without question. When you know you are always loved, there's nothing at risk. You get to be yourself, because you are loved, no matter what. You aren't depending on anyone else to love you to prove your worth. You *know* you are worthy. You *know* that you deserve whatever you desire, because you trust your inner knowing to be your guide.

The beauty disconnect happens when the lines get unplugged—when you stop loving your true self because you stop *seeing* your true self.

I WAS RECENTLY at a three-day retreat with 50 other powerful women. As soon as I got there, my mind started sizing everyone up.

That girl is really pretty. I wonder if she's also successful. I wonder if she's self-made or if she comes from money.

Damn, she's taking some serious notes. I bet she's really smart. She probably has the hottest boyfriend, too.

OMG, she looks flawless. Look at her jewelry! I bet she's a multimillionaire. But is she cool to hang out with?

All of a sudden, I started feeling insecure. I was in such

high judgment mode about everyone else that I was beginning to judge myself, too. I'd showed up to the event in my head and hadn't dropped into my body at all. For a moment, I got so wrapped up in who was there and how they looked that I wasn't connecting to my purpose and why *I* was there.

Your level of self-connection has nothing to do with how much you spend on beauty treatments. It doesn't matter whether you have your plastic surgeon on speed dial or have never set foot in a nail salon. It's about authenticity, integrity and connection. It's about knowing who you are on the inside and finding ways to bring that person to life on the outside.

You can be checking in at the med spa and still be completely *checked out* of your life. On the contrary, you can be checked in to your choices and crystal clear on why you just spent $800 to lighten the bags under your eyes. Every moment you feel yourself check out is a chance to check back in. It's an opportunity to get real with yourself. The disconnect will happen again, but the power to come back to yourself lies within you. The antidote for disconnection is simply connection—with yourself, your body and the person you see staring back at you in the mirror.

TWENTY-ONE

ENOUGH IS ENOUGH

"Whenever I feel bad, I use that feeling to motivate me to work harder. I only allow myself one day to feel sorry for myself. When I'm not feeling my best I ask myself, 'What are you gonna do about it?' I use the negativity to fuel the transformation into a better me."

—Beyoncé Knowles

"If you or a loved one have lost interest in hobbies and activities, you may want to call your doctor," the voiceover said.

In 2015, shortly after my brother Bo's death, I watched a TV commercial for antidepressants and thought, *Do I not want to shop because I'm depressed?*

After I left New York City and moved back to D.C., I was hyper-focused on my looks because I felt so physically terrible. Retail therapy was the only therapy I really believed in back then—until Bo died and I had to shop for funeral clothes. After that dark experience, I felt allergic to shopping. If buying things wouldn't bring him back, what was the point?

After the commercial ended, I closed my eyes and imagined myself walking into Bloomingdale's with Mom and Gram like in the old days. Did that make me feel anything? No.

What if it was Saks Fifth Avenue? I asked myself. Nope.

What if it was Saks Fifth Avenue on *Fifth Avenue?* Nothing. Totally numb.

I challenged myself one last time. I imagined walking through some of the most beautiful places I'd ever shopped. In my mind, I wove through the streets of Soho. I placed myself in the middle of Rodeo Drive. I walked the streets of Florence and Paris.

No matter how beautiful the location, I still didn't feel like shopping.

I had thought depression meant giving up and staying in bed all day, but I was getting up every morning to lead self-help workshops and coach other women. My businesses were growing. I was going through the motions, but something didn't feel right.

After seeing this commercial, it hit me: *I'm depressed.*

TODAY, I still use my desire to shop as a measure of my mental health. I shop when I travel, I shop online between meetings and I shop with my new boyfriend, who also loves to shop. When I'm shopping, I know that things are going pretty well.

At times, my love for buying beautiful things has gone too far, ultimately revealing itself as a sign of my own overfocus on external measures of happiness and success. When I was engaged to my ex, material things were among the many distractions that kept me in an increasingly dangerous situation. The Christmas that Jesse proposed, he gave me Louis Vuitton carry-on luggage and black suede Christian Louboutin over-the-knee boots—my first pair of red bottoms. Then, he asked for half of my company. This was how it worked. Almost every day, there was some sort of gift or surprise, but just as frequently, there was also some fight or drama.

When that relationship dissolved, I made enough through my designer resale account to cover a few mortgage payments, but I couldn't believe how much I had let material items sway me from my intuition. I'd always loved beautiful things. But when Jesse came into my life, I became a full-on material girl in a *delusional* world. In the wake of my long-term Lyme and my brother's passing, my priorities got warped.

When Jesse and I broke up, I sold everything he'd ever bought me. I sold everything I'd bought myself that reminded me of him. I needed to cleanse myself of his existence, reassess my values and move on.

Eventually, I found balance in this area of my life, reclaiming my love for shopping and even sliding my feet into a few new pairs of Valentinos. In this new phase, my goal was to ensure that my love for shopping and beautiful things never went away (it was part of me), but never drove me down a dark path again.

Sometimes, I felt alone in my search towards having it all. Just after I started my final round of Lyme treatment in June 2017, I met a new role model, someone who I could really look up to. I'd been praying for a new teacher for quite some time. There is a saying that when a student is ready, the teacher appears.

"I JUST WANT to feel *really* sexy," I told Brianna during one of our weekly appointments.

I'd hired Brianna as an acupuncturist, but it didn't take me long to understand that I'd also gotten a spiritual teacher.

A few years had passed since Bo's death and the breakup from hell. My hair was blonder and my forehead was tighter (thanks to Dysport because Botox gives me headaches). I'd dropped weight, emotionally and physically, and felt ready to show my curves.

"I think you do look sexy," Brianna said as she giggled at me, as she often did.

"Are you sure I shouldn't get my lips done?" I asked her. I'd always been obsessed with extra plump, juicy lips, and they were *really* having a moment.

"You don't want to look fake and you don't want to look out of reach to people," Brianna told me.

Brianna was an acupuncturist, an author and a local celebrity my friends and I referred to as "the lady with the silver hair." She embodied natural beauty. Her silver hair sparkled and the way she owned it was inspiring. Years before, I'd put a similar-looking woman on one of my vision boards. So, when I finally *met* the lady with the silver hair, I was in awe.

More importantly, I trusted Brianna because she was happy, which was what I wanted most of all. I felt safe being honest with her and felt I could tell her anything without being judged. I was in a place of transition, two years out from my brother's passing and fresh out of my treatment program. I could feel myself on the brink of understanding the next-level me. I was becoming and unbe-coming, finally evolving into my next iteration.

Brianna had a point. I *did* want to look good, but I didn't want to look fake. Where was the line? *Maybe I can chill with the beauty stuff for a minute,* I thought. *Maybe I finally look good enough.*

After this conversation, I put a pause on major beauty investments. Instead of plumping my lips, freezing my fore-head or researching plastic surgeons for a second nose job (because I wasn't totally happy with the first), I scaled back, channeling my beauty budget into surface-level Sephora shopping sprees over more invasive treatments.

For the moment, enough was enough.

TWENTY-TWO

TOUGH BUT BEAUTIFUL

"Behind every beautiful thing, there's been some kind of pain."
—Bob Dylan

Every morning, women everywhere wake up and face the music of their lives. Regardless of what drama is going on in the background, what size jeans they're fitting into or what age bracket they're in, they have to confront the truth and accept what's real. No matter which loved ones are sick, what stressors are happening at work, what's falling apart at home or what pain they feel in their bodies, minds or hearts, women take it on with beauty and grace. They take *all* of it on.

But not before swiping on some thick-ass mascara, right? Even after declaring that enough was enough with my own major beauty investments, I was swiping on some thick-ass mascara.

Women are survivors and providers. They radiate, shine

and glow. But with all this light, there's still a dark side, because most women don't tell the truth about what it takes to show up the way they do. They hide the truth of their late nights at work, their two-hour beauty routines, their juggling the partner and the kids and the endless striving for perfection. They can't relax unless there's weed or wine—maybe—and all of that is too temporary anyway.

When I was studying at Vanderbilt, I minored in Women's and Gender Studies. In one class, we studied *The Beauty Myth: How Images of Beauty Are Used Against Women* by Naomi Wolf, published in 1991. Wolf put words to what I'd felt since I was a teen:

> If a woman loves her own body, she doesn't
>   grudge what other women do with
>   theirs; if she loves femaleness, she
>   champions its rights. It's true what they
>   say about women: Women are
>   insatiable. We are greedy. Our appetites
>   do need to be controlled if things are to
>   stay in place. If the world were ours too,
>   if we believed we could get away with
>   it, we would ask for more love, more sex,
>   more money, more commitment to
>   children, more food, more care. These
>   sexual, emotional, and physical
>   demands would begin to extend to
>   social demands: payment for care of the
>   elderly, parental leave, childcare, etc.
>   The force of female desire would be so
>   great that society would truly have to
>   reckon with what women want, in bed
>   and in the world.

Although this resonated with me deeply, I'm not going to pretend I don't filter my photos. When I'm feeling particularly anxious, I start smoothing and straightening. It's not right, but it *is* real. And this is the major tension that so many women experience—a gut understanding that the expectations placed on external beauty are harmful and unjust and a mystifying instinct to play along anyway. Sometimes looking good becomes a coping mechanism—the one thing we can control when we can't control anything at all.

———

"TURN AROUND, Katie! Let's see the whole thing!" Gram would say.

When I was growing up, Sundays were for shopping—after church, of course. My mom would drive me and Gram to Bloomingdale's. We'd fill the dressing room with the latest trends for me to try on and I'd walk the hallway of the dressing room like a runway model.

I simultaneously loved and hated my family's emphasis on appearances. Throughout my teen years, the love-hate relationship grew more complicated. My brothers and I started going to fancy family dinners with my grandparents in Washington, D.C.

"Let's see what you've got on tonight!" Grandad would say, giving me and my perfectly accessorized outfit a once-over. I would twirl around, usually showing off some ensemble Gram and I had picked out the weekend before.

Gram and Grandad were a stylish power couple. They owned a well-known local business, and people in the D.C. area knew them and often said hello when we were out in the city. Looking good was important to them, and the message I received from them—along with my parents—was that if you looked good, you would feel good, too.

Given this family history, it shouldn't come as a surprise that the last word my grandfather whispered to me before he passed in October 2018 was *beautiful*.

It was the last word he said. Period.

———

MY MOM, Gram and I had spent the previous night in the king-size bed my grandparents had shared for almost 60 years. Grandad was next to us in the hospice bed he'd reluctantly moved to weeks prior. All night, we listened as he breathed heavily. The morphine was kicking in. We knew what was going to happen—and soon—but that didn't make it any easier. Death, like life, is unpredictable.

None of us slept much that night. The three of us tossed, turned and giggled nervously, popping up to make sure Grandad was still breathing when he got quiet for too long. When Gram got out of bed just before 6 am, she jumped right into her morning routine, slipping on the house shoes she'd worn for years, flip flopping noisily through the house, making her coffee and running her bath. No matter how dark the situation, there was no sleeping in. Life was going on.

Every day, I knew we were getting closer to *the* day and my anxiety grew exponentially. The occasional one milligram dose of Lorazepam was no longer cutting it. My stomach had been in knots for weeks as I waited for the inevitable news, so I'd scheduled a massage appointment about 15 minutes down the road from my grandparents' house that morning. I felt bad leaving, but my mom was heading to the office for a few hours. Gram seemed to be taking the day by the reins, too. My body and mind both needed to relax. The only way I could think to get rid of the anxiety was to have it massaged out of me.

Aware that it could be one of our last mornings with Grandad, I rolled out of bed and went into Gram's powder room to put on skinny jeans and a cozy cashmere sweater. I applied a light layer of foundation, added a few swipes of bronzer and blush, lined my lips and eyes, threw on some mascara and finished the look with my signature nude rose Yves Saint Laurent lip stain.

At least I look good, I thought to myself. It also made me feel a little better after a sleepless night. And it felt like a sign of respect. In my family, looking presentable for each other is what we do.

I walked into my grandparents' room and straight to Grandad's bedside.

"Good morning, handsome!" I said, holding onto the rails of his hospice bed and forcing a giant smile.

Grandad turned to me with sad, longing eyes. They lit up when he realized it was me. He cracked a smile, but it was a sad one.

"It's okay," I said as I looked at him and smiled wider. "You're doing great!" I wanted to look happy to ease his pain, but I could feel what was happening and I was terrified.

"I'm going to go out. I'll be right back," I told him.

Grandad looked me square in the eyes. "Beau-ti-ful," he whispered, just barely.

My heart expanded. I kissed him goodbye and told him I would see him later.

ALONG WITH BEING a savvy businessman and the founder of a nationally renowned fencing company, my grandad was a great adventurer, a phenomenal tennis player and an elegant ballroom dancer. He was captivating, hysterically funny and generous—the most highly respected man I ever knew. He loved hearing jokes and loved to play them on us, too. Once, when I was at his house for the afternoon, he dressed up in a yellow raincoat, put ketchup all over his arms and hid outside the kitchen window. When I first saw him, I was petrified, but when I couldn't find Grandad in the house, I had him figured out. What looked like a bloody intruder was my 70-something-year-old grandfather wearing Heinz 57 and a mustard yellow raincoat. Later, he asked if I'd seen the Boogeyman. I lied and told him I hadn't, because if he knew that his practical joke had worked, he was bound to do it again.

My brothers and I were the youngest grandchildren in the family. After us, there were great-grandchildren being born almost every year. As our family grew in size, so did Grandad's audience. Every Christmas, he dressed up as a politician, celebrity or historical figure—Ronald Regan, Bill Clinton, John Gotti and even one of the guys from *Duck Dynasty*.

Grandad was so extra. It's the only way to describe him.

He taught me everything: how to bait a fishing line, how to do a figure-eight on a jet ski and how to get the right shot in tennis. He taught me how to make money, save money and invest in myself and my business. He taught me how to invest in the stock market. He was a foodie before foodies existed, schooling us about how to enjoy fine dining, keep our elbows off the table and put our napkins in our laps. He told me my education was the one thing no one could ever take away from me, which I now know was inspired by singer-songwriter B.B. King.

Most importantly, Grandad showed me how to be generous, how to love and how to live. He was—and to me, still is—everything: timeless, ageless and ever-present. He was the kind of man I never thought would die, and even though I can't *see* him anymore, I know he's still here with us. It helps that I see signs with the name of his fence company on nearly every block of the nation's capital, which also happens to be my hometown. For the rest of my life, he'll be sending me signs from the other side.

———

I HOLD on to his memory in other ways, too. Just 10 days before that sleepless night next to his hospice bed, my parents and I spent a Saturday afternoon with Gram and Grandad. It was one of my grandfather's most lucid final days. While I was sitting with him, I turned on my phone's voice recorder and tucked it behind me so no one would see. I caught some final moments that make me both laugh *and* cry, like only the most precious memories can. Grandad was trying to get me—his gluten-free, dairy-free granddaughter —to eat broccoli and cheese soup from Panera Bread.

"Did you try this soup? It's so good it's obscene," he said.

"No, I'm okay," I replied.

"What do you mean you're okay?" he said.

"I don't feel like eating," I said.

"I didn't ask you how you felt," he said.

I laughed. "I can't eat cheese. Is it good?"

"Succulent," he said. I laughed again. That—along with

"it's so good it's obscene"—was one of his favorite ways to describe food.

When I play the recording now, I laugh and picture the scene around the broccoli and cheese soup. My dad and I are propping him up with stacks of pillows so he can sit up in bed. Gram is arranging the room to make space for the newly added oxygen tank. Grandad is recounting how Gram cursed at him the night before for trying to climb out of his hospice bed. Grandad mentions he's lost his full memory and that my dad is definitely spending too much money. He tells us he's not ready to leave his beautiful family.

We also talked about lighter things like Grandad's mediocre babysitting skills. Once, he took me to swimming lessons but then couldn't find me because a random woman was braiding my hair in the women's locker room. Then there was the time he left me to babysit seven great-grandkids at his summer house, scheduled landscapers without telling me and left without warning. I locked all the doors, shut all the blinds and made everyone lie on the floor. I thought they were strangers trying to break in, and since I couldn't find Grandad, I thought they had gotten him first. I was 11 years old and too young to legally babysit, but Grandad loved to force independence and survival skills on us.

"You really gave your grandkids a strong start in life," my dad said to Grandad.

"Well, like I told Johnny yesterday, when you start with nothing—and I started with nothing—it's a great feeling to give," Grandad said.

Between deep coughs, reminding us all of the esophageal cancer, we discussed investment strategies, charity, stocks and profit margins. Grandad shared the story of pursuing my grandmother for what would be the final time. At one point, out of nowhere, he looked at me and said, "You have beautiful teeth and beautiful eyes."

I thanked him. My heart was breaking and expanding all at once.

WHILE I WAS LOOKING for a parking spot outside my massage appointment, my phone rang. It was Gram. She said that Grandad had just passed, moments after I left. It was as if he was waiting for me to go to have his final moment with her.

I could already feel her mix of deep peace in letting him go and the even deeper heartbreak of losing the man she had loved for over half a century. Together, they'd built an amazing business that touched so many lives and a wonderful family that had grown well beyond their living room. It didn't matter who was hosting Christmas on any given year. Family events had become standing room only. It had all started with them.

"I got to hold him as he passed, Katie," Gram said. "The nurses called me in, and I was right there with him."

She sounded so amazingly grateful for that final scene.

I told Gram I would be right there, but first, I sat in my car, frozen. There it was. That was the ending. I thought back to our final moments and his last word: *beautiful*. It was one word, but it meant so much. Our family was beautiful. I was beautiful. This life was truly beautiful.

I never got a final moment with my brother, Bo. You can imagine how much I needed that final moment with my grandfather. Even through all my awkward tween years, when he'd sit outside the tennis courts in scalding summer temperatures and yell at me to run to the ball, he always told me I was beautiful. Even when I was soaked in water with a swim cap on, getting out of the pool at swim practice or covered in worm guts from fishing all day, he'd sing our song: "K-K-K-Katie, beautiful Katie, I'll be knocking at the k-k-k-kitchen door!"

And knock on the kitchen door—covered in ketchup —he did.

Even with the expectations my family set around looking good and the complicated feelings I'd had about them over the years, I knew my grandfather's compliments were never just about physical beauty. He could see both inner *and* outer beauty. He saw that I was tough, but beautiful—true beauty at its core.

PART FOUR
BOYS

TWENTY-THREE
DADDY ISSUES

"She is a reflection of all the people she wants to love."

—R.M. Drake

My dad is the best.

My dad is smart, charismatic, successful and super generous. Six feet tall and dark-haired, he's pretty good-looking, too. And to top it off, he's funny as hell. At any opportunity, he'll have the whole table laughing hysterically. Making people laugh is his thing. My dad has big, bright eyes and a giant smile, just like me, but his powerful presence comes from more than just his physical appearance.

It's my dad's *vibe* that makes him stand out. Something about him feels inspiring, expansive, comforting and steady all at once. When you're with him, you have a sense that he's got you. You're going to be okay and so is everything else.

I'm not just saying this because I'm his daughter or even his *only* daughter. Everyone who meets my dad and really gets to know him feels this way.

Having such a great guy as my dad has influenced me in many different ways, but it's especially affected how I approach the dating game, a game I've now been playing for over 20 years. I wouldn't say I have daddy issues per se, but I would admit to having one *single* issue: My relationship with my dad is so great that I can't help but compare every guy to my father.

The thing about having a great dad is that all you ever want is to meet someone like him.

If you've spent any time online dating, you know how tricky it can be. Texting is the new normal, no one knows how to make a phone call and charisma is drying up faster than you can say "global warming." Modern dating is like looking for a needle in a haystack, particularly when you're trying to find a partner to measure up to a great parent.

When I was growing up, the best thing about my dad was that he really believed in me. He helped me with my schoolwork and coached my sports teams. He drove me to school in the mornings. We listened to Tony Robbins cassette tapes on the way. As soon as we got in the car, the track he'd been listening to the night before would start playing.

"Leave it on," I'd say. "I want to listen."

Tony taught us both *How to Shape Your Destiny Now* and *How to Get What You Really Want*. Clearly, I got my early love for self-help from my father. My dad said the possibilities were endless. He urged me to dream big. He also wanted me to be with a certain type of someone, and as I grew out of those carpool days, he was rarely a fan of the guys I brought home.

I learned a lot from my dad about what I deserve. The standards he set weren't always specific, like "a man should pay for dinner." It was more general, like "a man should do the right thing." Even though I asked for them, my dad wouldn't give me a specific set of rules. He'd say things like "Trust yourself" and "You'll know when you find it."

AS MY BROTHERS GET OLDER—JOHNNY, now a father himself, and Bo in spirit, still looking out for me—I think about what I learned from them, too.

Johnny was always the protector. Since he and I barely resemble each other, people would often think we were dating. If I was with Johnny and another guy tried to talk to me, Johnny would give him a look that sent him running to the other side of the room. When it came to bringing my boyfriends home, Johnny was worse than my dad.

Bo, on the other hand, was the lover. He once made a video for a girlfriend of himself lip-syncing Chicago's "If You Leave Me Now." We rediscovered it after he passed. The clip made its way into his memorial video on YouTube. The lyrics describe how his loved ones felt when he left.

If you leave me now, you'll take away the biggest part of me.

No, baby, please don't go.

A love like ours is love that's hard to find.

How could we let it slip away?

We've come too far to leave it all behind.

How could we end it all this way?

Bo must have been 12 or 13 when he made the video, which should show you just how much of a lover he was, even at a young age. I still remember the names of all his girlfriends—and there were many. His funeral was sprinkled with girls in their late teens and early 20s, some polished and preppy, others covered with tattoos, sniffling their way through the ceremony and hugging me, my parents and Johnny on their way out.

Together, my brothers taught me that I deserved a partner who was both a protector and a lover—and protection and love were equally important. My dad is the best. My grandad was extra. Together, the men in my family set a super high standard.

TWENTY-FOUR

MIXED MESSAGES

"Maybe some women aren't meant to be tamed. Maybe they need to run free until they find someone just as wild to run with them."
—Carrie Bradshaw, *Sex and the City*

"It hurts so bad, Dad," I told him through tears.

"It will hurt for a little bit, but you'll get through it. You're strong," he said.

"I hate boys."

"They aren't all terrible," he said. "Someday, you'll meet someone who will be your rock." My dad was often prophetic like this.

"I just want to find someone like you." I buried my face in his shoulder, sobbing hysterically. My eyes were puffy. I'd been crying for hours.

"You will, Katie. You will."

There I was, 14 years old, crying on my dad's shoulder over the 16-year-old prick who I knew he'd never liked in the first place. And there was Dad, patting my head, handing me tissues and trying to get me to breathe between words.

I'd dated Kyle for two years, which is a lifetime in a teen relationship. It was the summer before my sophomore year of high school. Kyle was just one grade ahead of me, but two years older, so dating him made me feel sophisticated and mature. I loved driving around in his Jeep and meeting his older friends at our Catholic high school.

Kyle was deep and different, with a bit of a dark side. One day, he surprised me with a tiny diamond ring, which he placed on my right hand. Later, he put it on my left ring finger and said, "Someday, I'm going to get you an even bigger one for this finger." I believed it and so did my friends.

As it turned out, Kyle had been cheating on me with a skinny blonde who went to a nearby public school. Never one to avoid a direct conversation, I found her and got to know her myself on AOL Instant Messenger. A first breakup is bound to be painful, but add a side of infidelity and you've got a serious punch to the gut.

I stayed in my room for days after the breakup. I didn't know how to open up to my friends. Kyle was the one I would typically go to when I was sad, but now he was the *reason* I was hurting. After all, it had been good before it got bad. He once left roses, chocolate and a stuffed animal in my locker. Everyone knew he was super romantic, but now I felt ashamed and embarrassed about all of it. How would I explain this to my friends?

After a few days of nonstop tears, Kyle and I finally talked. He put the blame on me, of course. He said that messaging his blonde mistress online to get the dirt on what happened made me seem insecure. Really, it just made me a detective. Even at 14, I was very resourceful.

But there was another piece of the story that left me feeling even more traumatized. A few months earlier, Kyle had been going through a tough time. In hindsight, I realize he must have been struggling with depression, but since my family didn't talk about mental health back then, I didn't know what depression was. One night, Kyle told me he loved me so much that if I ever broke up with him, he would want to die, even if that meant killing himself.

I was confused by Kyle's profession of love. On the one hand, it was powerful. On the other, it was tragic. *You love me so much that you can't live without me?* To my hopelessly romantic 14-year-old self, it felt part *Romeo and Juliet* and part *really* wrong. The moment he said it, I felt a pinch in the pit of my stomach. I felt obligated to take care of Kyle and avoid hurting him at all costs, even at my own expense.

Kyle claimed he was only expressing his unconditional love. But really, it was the most conditional.

I had thought I was supposed to marry this boy, but after it ended, I felt used. I didn't want other people to see my pain, so I did my best to handle it on my own. My dad had another plan, though. At the time, most of my friends were confiding in their moms about their crushes and boy problems, but it was my dad who came to the rescue for me.

It was the first breakup my dad walked me through and it definitely wouldn't be the last. Thanks to Dad's ability to remind me of who I am and source my inner strength, I've made it through some nasty splits, mostly in one piece. But I never stopped worrying about whether I'd find someone as great as my dad. I worried about it for decades.

I spent years looking for the perfect romantic partner who would have my dad's best qualities. And I spent years trying to act, dress and look like my mom. But I'm not my mom. I'm me. I can be a lot to handle and most people can't keep up. They aren't deep enough, free enough or brave enough. Most people don't see the world the way I do.

I've modeled myself after my parents, yes, but even they don't get it.

MY PARENTS MET during my mom's freshman year of college. She was 17 and he was 18. It was Mom's freshman retreat. Dad was a sophomore and a student counselor. According to Mom, it was love at first sight. She still tells the story of the day they met, sat on the fence and talked about what they wanted for the future—not together, necessarily, but from the beginning, they shared their dreams and realized they were quite similar. Soon after that, they started dating and continued throughout college. They once got locked in the library together when they were up late studying. They kissed in the back of the campus church. Mom says Dad would come over to her dorm room to hang out and fall asleep immediately because he was working two jobs and exhausted, but still had to see her.

There was no doubt about it—they were completely in love.

They graduated, got engaged, got married, had me and started their MBAs. I was at their business school graduation, and since they shared the same last name by then, they walked the stage together to receive their diplomas. I walked with them. It's all pretty cute.

As far back as I can remember, I saw my parents making moves together. To me, that seemed like the definition of partnership.

The refrigerator in our family's first townhouse had a wooden magnet that said, "Happiness is being married to your best friend," surrounded by hand-painted flowers. That pretty much captured it. As a kid, I stared at that magnet, which stayed on the fridge through two moves and 30 years. I figured a best friendship must be the key to a long-term romantic relationship, and it became what I ultimately wanted from my own partner. Thanks to that magnet, I was on a mission to find my best friend and marry him.

MOM WAS REALLY happy when I started dating Mikey in high school, even if Johnny thought he was lame and Bo was still too young to have an opinion. I'm not exactly sure what my dad thought of him, but everyone in my family could see Mikey was a departure from Kyle—and that was a good thing. For starters, he was Italian and Catholic, which to my parents, at least, meant he came from a good family. I hoped it would mean he'd be a lot more like my dad, too.

I was a sophomore in high school when I started hanging out with Mikey. I was running for student government vice president, and since Mikey played varsity lacrosse and football, I asked him to be my campaign manager so I could get the athlete vote. It was a strategic move. Having Mikey as my hype man worked. I won.

By the time I went back to school for my junior year to serve as vice president, Mikey and I were officially dating. It had gone from political to personal pretty fast. I'd liked him from the start and the fact that he drove to my parents' house after practice and helped me work on my election day speech made me fall for him even harder. Like my dad,

Mikey was smart and cool and he believed in me. He wasn't making a clear move, so for a long time, I didn't know if it was more than friendship for him. Eventually, Mikey and I got together. My senior year, we were voted "class couple" in the yearbook. We went to different colleges and kept dating for four and a half years.

We broke up the week I left to study abroad in Australia. I was visiting him at Bucknell University, where he played NCAA Division I lacrosse. It was Valentine's Day weekend, and since he couldn't come visit while I was abroad because of his lacrosse schedule, it would be the last time I'd see him for six months.

"I want you to have the time of your life, but I want you to come back to me," he said.

I nodded my head and smiled. It was the most romantic thing anyone had ever said to me, and it didn't have any tragic *Romeo and Juliet* vibes. At 20 years old, it felt like the purest love there could be. But there was something missing with Mikey. I was deeply craving something that I couldn't put my finger on. The only thing I knew for sure was that I had to go to Australia. It felt like there was a physical force pulling me to get there, so even though it meant putting my relationship on hold, I went. I drove away from our Valentine's Day weekend as a single woman, knowing Mikey would be waiting for me.

As soon as I landed in Australia, everything became instantly clear. What I had been craving was adventure. Mikey didn't want any part of that. In fact, when I'd told him I wanted to live in Washington, D.C. after college— instead of in Annapolis, which was only 30 miles away—he told me he'd never leave our hometown.

Not long after arriving in Australia, I met someone new. His name was Vinny. He was another Italian and a native New Yorker and our attraction was instant. We sat across from each other at lunch, sat next to each other during orientation and ended up at the same bar on our first night, all by total coincidence—or rather, magnetism. When we walked home together at 2 am, we realized we were living next door to each other.

There was a powerful energy between me and Vinny that I hadn't experienced before. We also had a lot in common. Like me, he'd just broken up with someone from home. We bonded over our similar situations. It was clear we liked each other a lot, but we decided to hang out, have fun and not put too much pressure on defining the relationship, since the whole point of both of us being single in Australia was to be single in Australia.

I appreciated the new sense of freedom. I was single, studying abroad and spending time with a total stud. But not being in a committed relationship also started to fuel my fear of being alone forever. I was 20. If I was going based on the timeline of my parents' love story, I should have fallen in love with my future husband three years earlier. Even though Vinny and I promised to keep things pressure-free, the pressure was still on in the back of my mind. I couldn't help but wonder if this Italian stallion would be the one to make all my relationship dreams come true.

Was I meant to find true love in Australia?

The answer was yes.

A great love story went down while I was Down Under, but it wasn't with Vinny. This was a self-love love story.

———

IN AUSTRALIA, I met the next version of myself. There was something about the energy of that entire continent that felt open, expansive and full of possibility. While I was there, something activated within me—a creative energy and an innate sexiness, a desire and a lust for life. Going abroad was the most independent, self-loving move I had ever made.

But even though I loved who I became in Australia, I continued to worry that the power partnership I ultimately wanted would never exist. My early experiences with dating just kept proving my fears were real. I constantly questioned whether there was a man as perfect for me as my dad was for my mom. Looking back, I think the reason I was so afraid I'd never get what I wanted was simply that I didn't know if it was possible to have it. The most destructive fears come from doubting our instincts, our intuition and ourselves—and from questioning our visions of the future.

This is why the manifesting process I teach works so well. Once I started *believing* I could have anything I wanted, checking in to make sure my desires were aligned with my Greatest Level of Want and deciding I would have them, my entire world changed.

Ask yourself what you *really* want. Is there any part of you that doesn't believe you can have it? Is there any part of you that isn't sure you deserve it? Is there any part of you that worries you might be asking for too much?

Eventually, I taught myself how to see, feel, be and do my way to having everything I wanted. But back then, I was still Down Under trying to figure it all out. It would be almost a decade before I hacked the manifestation process and started to take my romantic destiny into my own hands.

Before I could attract a power partnership, I had to become powerful on my own.

TWENTY-FIVE

NEEDY IS AN ENERGY

"It was when I realized I needed to stop trying to be somebody else and be myself that I actually started to own, accept and love what I had."

—Tracee Ellis Ross

Text from me: *Soooo I moved to NYC*

Text from Vinny: *Were you going to tell me?*

Text from me: *I'm telling you now*

The gift in meeting Vinny was that he inspired me to move to New York, where I needed to be for the next chapter of my life to begin. To be clear, I didn't move there for him. In fact, I didn't even text him until I was sitting on the floor of the apartment that my best friend from college and I were sharing with some girl she sort of knew.

I'd always secretly hoped Vinny and I would work out. Our connection was so magnetic, I knew I'd never be bored with him. But the reality was that he was barely trying. With Vinny, I got into a cycle of trying to *win* at the dating game, putting in way too much effort, completely backing away and then beating myself up over the unrelenting pattern.

The movie *He's Just Not That Into You* came out around this time. It's based on a self-help book of the same name, written by Greg Behrendt and Liz Tuccillo. Even though it has an ensemble cast—Ben Affleck, Jennifer Aniston, Drew Barrymore, Bradley Cooper and Scarlett Johansson, to name a few—the movie, like the book, is extremely disempowering. If you haven't read or watched, here's a quick summary of the key takeaway: Unless a guy wants you and *only* you, drops all of his selfish ways and asks you to marry him, he's just not that into you.

I understand the core premise—to a point. If someone wants to be with you, you shouldn't have any doubts. They should make it clear. But what about the months—and often years—that go down between the first encounter and marriage? Real love develops over time. Starting a relationship expecting the other person to be all in from the get-go seems like an unfair bar to set, not to mention an unrealistic one.

There are other problems with the book, like its assumption that only heteronormative relationships exist and its overemphasis on a specific male-female dynamic in which men make all the decisions and all women do is respond to them. Plus, it presumes that it's always a *man's* uncertainty driving the split. What if a woman isn't sure about a guy?

The book and movie are meant to be self-help guides for single women, but I was a single woman and they weren't helping me at all. In fact, they were reinforcing many of the unhelpful (and unhealthy) rules I had learned in my first relationship with Kyle.

Rule 1: If a man wants you, he will chase you down.

Rule 2: If he doesn't chase you, he doesn't want you.

Rule 3: Relationships are predominantly about men.

These aren't *exactly* the rules laid out in the book and movie, but they were the rules I took from them.

I couldn't understand why the arbitrary "he" wouldn't be into me. I'm competitive, so after reading the book, I started to think that someone being into me was something I could change with persistence. If dating was a game, I was going to be the best at playing it. Whoever "he" was, he would be into me. I'd make sure of it. And if he wasn't, I'd bounce hard and make him feel as abandoned and embarrassed as he'd made me feel. At least I had a plan, right?

As soon as I told Vinny I was in New York City, I expected him to come running after me. I wanted him to chase me, prove he *was* into me and confirm that I was good enough to get him. Without realizing it, I had created an unhealthy dynamic of needing him to validate my self-worth.

After a while, though, I got tired of trying to get Vinny to want me. I was chasing him, not the other way around, so the whole *He's Just Not That Into You* approach didn't work for me at all. What it *did* teach me was that some men are truly unavailable—and I was dating one of them.

Vinny wasn't the first emotionally unavailable man I'd dated and he wouldn't be the last. Even after all these years, though, I don't think the real problem is ever emotional unavailability. Everyone is unavailable until the moment they become available.

It's a person's unwillingness to open up and *become* available that makes intimacy a challenge. The problem with a more stringent approach to dating is that if you refuse to spend time with or even be friends with an unavailable person, you might not get the memo when they finally free up. What if you're the exact inspiration they need to make themselves available?

There were things I liked about Vinny, and there were also things I saw in him that I wanted for myself—his confident vibe, his savvy New Yorker ways, his sense of style. I wanted to be more like that, but I didn't need him to do it for me. Being inspired by him was different from needing him.

I don't remember if Vinny and I ever officially ended things or if we just let it fade. Either way, he eventually ended up back with his girlfriend from home and I was back to square one, 22 years old, living in New York City and wondering if I would ever find my true soulmate. I had let Mikey go to pursue a new, more adventurous love, but since my new love wasn't pursuing me, I had to let him go, too.

WHAT IF GOD came down to Earth right now and told me I would meet my soulmate in exactly two years, three months and 15 days? If I knew that for sure, what would I do with my time now?

One day while walking around Gramercy Park, I got a wild download on dating. A download is an idea, piece of information or a spark of inspiration that lands in your brain, seemingly out of nowhere. Once it locks in, it makes total sense.

My answers to these questions blew me away.

I would find my true passion and figure out what I want to do with my life.

I would spend more time enjoying my friends without an agenda.

I would date for practice and start enjoying the experi-

ence of dating, rather than dreading it or trying to perform and win the game.

I would use my experiences with other men to get ready for my future partner.

It came down to this: If I could get certainty around my future, I would change my approach to life. This forced me to ask myself more questions.

How would I spend my time and energy if I wasn't wasting it worrying about finding the right guy? Would I eliminate certain people or activities from my circle? Could I finally focus on other things that really matter to me? How would I optimize my single years while also preparing to meet my true love?

If I fully knew my partner was coming and the date was set, I could stop worrying and just live my life. I dug deep in my heart. I knew my partner was coming. I had a divine desire to meet him, and it was coming from my Greatest Level of Want. If that was the case, there was no way it wouldn't be fulfilled. This gave me peace.

Around that time, I came across a quote from *A Course in Miracles* that says, "Those who are certain of the outcome can afford to wait and wait without anxiety."

That was the reframe I needed. Finally, I could start to manifest what I truly desired, trust that it was coming and ditch the worry once and for all. I decided I would have what I wanted. The only thing I didn't know for sure was *when* I would meet my person. I started to repeat this affirmation: *My soulmate is coming and will arrive at the ideal time.* Every day, I asked myself how I would operate if I had implicit knowledge that my partner was coming. Each time I asked, I got more clarity about what my next move should be.

The first step, I realized, was cleaning up my own needy energy.

During this period, I learned that if you truly want a relationship, you can't be in the energy of *needing* one. I think that's why so many people say you'll find a relationship as soon as you stop looking. For a lot of people, it's once they give up on love, throw their hands in the air and say, "I'd rather be alone than have to deal with this shit!" that a more evolved love actually comes their way. You have to be willing to walk away from anyone and anything that doesn't meet your desires, even if that means being alone.

Everyone talks about being needy like it's the worst thing in the world. But being needy is just a symptom of not knowing exactly what you need or how to get it on your own. It's important to recognize that you—not your partner —are responsible for meeting those needs.

Almost every time I ask a student, team member or friend what they need for the first time, they react strongly. *I don't know! Nothing. What do you mean?* Most people aren't intimately in touch with their needs because they simply aren't taught to connect with how they feel. In fact, most people are taught that needs are negative. Traditionally speaking, "needy" is not a good look.

But being needy is just the condition of having unmet needs and not knowing how to address them, so I'm here to tell you that needy isn't bad. It's just an energy.

When you're feeling needy, you're craving *something*. When you get curious about your feeling of neediness and explore what the sensation is telling you, you can get responsible, fill your own cup and get what you want out of life. Neediness isn't a fun place to hang out, but it only comes when your needs aren't being met. You have to listen to yourself.

Perhaps you need to feel beautiful or relaxed or healthy. Maybe you need to sleep or share what's on your mind. Maybe you need to be seen, heard or acknowledged. The more clearly you know what your needs are, the more easily you can get them met.

It's also worth mentioning the difference between needing and wanting. I *wanted* the relationships I've told you about so far to work out. That was true. But I also told myself I *needed* them to work. That was a lie.

Like all relationships, romantic relationships depend on the free will of others, so you don't know how they're going to pan out. I now practice non-attachment to any specific person or relationship while staying committed to my ultimate desire, which is always to be with the partner who's perfect for me. Once I got clear on that, I learned to keep it front and center in each situation. I couldn't forget my vision of a perfect partnership, but I had to stop holding onto it so tightly if I wanted to manifest it into reality.

Practicing non-attachment in love doesn't mean you avoid commitment or emotionally detach. In fact, it's the opposite. Attachment creates control and constriction, and since relationships need expansion and openness to grow, non-attachment can actually open the door to playing all in and being committed.

You're living in ultimate trust, remember? If you get to have what you want (and you do), then you don't have to worry about whether or not it's going to happen. *It's going to happen.*

TWENTY-SIX

THE FOUR MAN PLAN

"No matter where you are in life, you'll save a lot of time by not worrying too much about what other people think about you. The earlier in your life that you can learn that, the easier the rest of it will be."

—Sophia Amoruso

You *can* attract your soulmate and you *can* manifest your ideal relationship.

But you have to get real with yourself first.

Manifestation is the process of attracting what you want. But what do you want? If you're anything like me, that's difficult to answer, because you've grown up with so many messages about what you *should* and *shouldn't* want in your life. You might even think you know what you want, but when you get honest with yourself, you see it's coming from the lens of what you *don't* want. That's not enough to manifest your way into your ideal future.

Stop looking at what you *don't* want. Take time to envision the person and the partnership you *do* want. Ask yourself how it will *feel* when you attract your ideal relationship or when your current relationship evolves to the next level.

Once you connect with the *feeling* of the person and the partnership, you can recognize it when it arrives. You have to practice finding through feeling. If a connection doesn't *feel* the way you know your ideal relationship is supposed to feel, either it isn't the right relationship or the relationship needs to evolve.

When I was in my early 20s, working long hours and searching for my person at hotel bars and on dating apps, I wasn't thinking about love in this way, and I definitely wasn't aware of all the relationship rules I follow now. The funny thing about dating during this period was that God kept sending me men who were just a *little* wrong for me. They were interesting but a little condescending, hysterical but a little unmotivated, successful but a little dishonest, loving but a little unattractive.

I was seeing all the attributes I wanted, but not in one person. So, I kept dating. All of them.

"THERE'S this one guy who's cute, but he seems a little wild," I said. "There's another who's been flirting me up in the snack room, and there's another I'm still talking to who I used to date in college." I was referring to Vinny, of course.

"Oh my God! You have to do the Four Man Plan!" Charlie said. "You're basically doing it now."

Charlie pulled out his notebook and quickly sketched a diagram. He drew a square and broke it down into four quadrants. He then divided all of the quadrants again.

The Four Man Plan

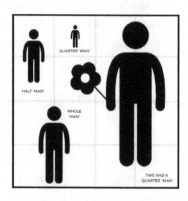

"You date four guys at a time," he said. "They move through the boxes based on how they're showing up for you. You don't sleep with anyone. Wait, I think you can actually sleep with the guy in the two boxes to the right. When they impress you, you move them to a bigger box and when you're over it, you take them off the chart and find your new number four."

Charlie was my best friend at my new job and *The Four Man Plan* was another relationship self-help book. Charlie had been doing the plan himself since moving to New York City. He clearly trusted it. And since he was gay and my only work friend who wasn't trying to sleep with me, I trusted him.

It was perfect, because in my early phase of learning not to be needy, I wasn't sure if I even *wanted* just one person. The odds were in my favor with the Four Man Plan. If one backed out, there were still three more waiting, and if they all backed out, I knew where to find another set of four—at my new office, which was full of prospective candidates.

The Four Man Plan saved me. It gave me an exact roadmap for dating. Rather than getting played, I became the player. My destiny was in *my* hands, not Mikey's or Vinny's or anyone else's.

One of the plan's rules was to say yes to every invitation. That way, you'd open yourself to the possibility that anyone could turn out to be the one for you. This got me out of my comfort zone.

According to the plan, "the one" wasn't actually the one. He didn't fill up all four quadrants—and he wasn't expected to. The one was your three-and-a-half man. He filled up three and a half of the boxes. That final half represented the importance of fulfilling your own needs. This appealed to my growing identity as an increasingly empowered woman. It was all starting to add up—literally.

Contrary to the premise of *He's Just Not That Into You* —which focused on a prospective man's agenda over my own—this approach was about whether or not *I* was into *him*. It also didn't require total obsession from either person, which was a relief. The new strategy left plenty of space for trial and error. I could screw up, choose the wrong person and it would all be okay. There would always be three more right there, and many others were just a casual meeting away. My dating world opened up and the opportunities were endless.

Another rule turned out to be really helpful for me. Whether or not I initially liked a man, I had to give him two dates, unless, of course, he was a total red flag. The author of *The Four Man Plan,* Cindy Lu, said that over half of women who were happy in their relationships admitted to initially not liking their partners. Not liking someone from the get-go also shifted the dating dynamic in those first few dates. If I didn't even *like him,* I definitely wasn't convincing myself I *needed him.*

This perspective helped me continue developing my

main relationship rule: If you truly want a relationship, you can't be in the energy of needing one. Having four men at a time helped eliminate the needy energy I was trying to avoid.

Charlie taught me how to collect my men and what they had to do to move their way through the quadrants to eventually become "the one" (aka the three-and-a-half man). Now, instead of trying to fit myself into a box to keep a prospective partner, I was collecting them like Louis Vuitton bags and moving them through the plan.

I didn't understand why I'd waited so long to be a player. It wasn't an aggressive game, but rather one of experimenting, experiencing and seeing what was out there. My neediness lessened because with four prospects, I needed less from each one. Also, having four meant my expectations of each were lowered. In the process, I learned to rely more on myself.

Dating like it was a game helped me survive and taught me more about myself. But when it came down to it, I didn't want to win the game just to score a lover. I wanted to meet my soulmate and be part of a power couple. Eventually, I realized if I wanted a chance at real love, I had to stop being so focused on winning. I had to become willing to lose, and with that, to let go.

For me, letting go didn't just mean being the cool girl who could say she didn't care or would always go with the flow. I had to simultaneously be *in* my relationships—by showing up and being vulnerable—and then let go by allowing space for the relationship to breathe. Letting go of my attachment to the outcomes of my romantic relationships was the key to my internal shift. It was also the most expansive, freeing choice I could have made.

In letting go, I started to surrender my will and ask for

divine intervention. It wasn't a submission. It was an opening. Because I deeply believed I was destined to be in partnership, I'd spent so much time and energy trying to force things that never belonged to me in the first place. My past relationships hadn't necessarily failed because we weren't right for each other. They'd failed because I wanted them to work so badly that I was willing to force them at all costs. Whether or not it was meant for me, I was so committed to having what I thought I needed that I accepted things from myself and the people I dated that were not up to my standards.

A Course in Miracles says, "Make your romantic relationships more brotherly and your friendships more romantic." I found this passage during a breakup and took it seriously. I wrote love letters to my friends. I planned surprises for family members. I didn't need a partner to be in love. I could be in love with life itself.

LOVE COMES IN ALL FORMS, and I started to realize it was abundant. Whether I was dating one person or four, if I couldn't get the love I desired and if the dynamics were highlighting my needy energy, I could just source the love I needed from somewhere else. I could source love from myself, both by giving and receiving it.

Eventually, I taught myself how to find love and romance in all areas of my life—with myself, my friendships, my work and my purpose. And it wasn't having four boyfriends to fill the void that set me free! It was realizing there wasn't a void to begin with. I didn't need anything except *me*. I was the source of everything I could ever want or need.

If you're anything like me, when you're constantly looking for your other half (or if you're in a relationship, trying to find yourself through your partner), you forget this one major truth: You're already whole.

The key to remembering this regardless of your relationship status is to *be* the source of love around you. Send handwritten cards to your clients, your kids, your best friend, your yoga teacher, your grandma or anyone else you love dearly. Give small, thoughtful gifts—not just on birthdays or holidays, but all throughout the year. Most importantly, be generous and give to yourself. At the core, you are the one you've been waiting for. The most important relationship you'll ever manifest is the one with yourself.

You're probably wondering whether any of those men from my Four Man Plan stuck. The answer is yes.

PJ and I fell quickly in love. This time, it was a different kind of love. There was a level of loyalty, understanding and a mysterious familiarity that I'd never experienced before.

PJ was different from any guy I'd ever known. He was spiritual and creative. He was a dreamer. We attracted, magnetized and manifested our way into each other's lives. The first time he told me he liked me, he said he was attracted to my energy. I had never heard that line from a guy before.

PJ talked about life, energy and the universe in a way that was brand new to me. He loved to talk about philosophy and share ideas. When I went to his apartment, I saw a book called *Money, and the Law of Attraction* on his bookshelf. I remembered seeing stacks of books about how to become a millionaire and live your best life in my parents' bathroom, on my dad's nightstand and strewn around my dad's gym in the basement, but PJ was interested in an entirely different path to becoming successful and getting rich. I didn't read the book back then, but many years later, I would circle back to it. The concepts of the Law of Attraction and manifesting would become a core part of my work and my teachings.

PJ felt like family, and I assumed he would be one day, legally speaking. But my needy energy reared its ugly head, and once I got into the relationship, I was afraid I'd lose it. Because I had never met anyone I'd connected with on such a deep level, I held onto the relationship even more tightly than I had to others in the past. I fought hard to make it work. In our own ways, we both fought for it. We moved from New York City to D.C. together. I started my spray tan business in our apartment. PJ helped me brainstorm names and transform a Wordpress blog into a working website so people could start scheduling appointments.

We bared our souls and shared our biggest dreams, but we were young, naive and both a bit selfish at our cores. Eventually, it became clear that we weren't matching up anymore. I wanted him to change for me, and he felt he'd never be able to make me happy. My fighting for the relationship turned into us fighting nonstop. A relationship is supposed to be charged, but with me and PJ, there was too much charge. Eventually, the power went out and we both had to let go. I was heartbroken that such a great love could turn so bad.

I learned a lot about love in that relationship with PJ. I learned when you love someone and go all in, you let them see all of you, which includes the parts that look good and the ones that don't. When you let yourself love so openly, you see *yourself* differently too. You get to experience new parts of who you are. With PJ, I saw myself in a new light. I started to see my energy, my presence and my power. It was transformative.

One rule I repeat constantly in both business and life is this: *What's meant for you can't miss you.* In fact, it will arrive at the perfect time.

The challenge is that you don't know when.

If God just showed up and told me I would have everything I desire from my G.L.O.W., my Greatest Level of Want, and gave me the specific day and time I would get it, I'd be calm, cool and collected. And if I knew those dates and times for sure, I would think seriously about how I wanted to spend the time before it happened. Although I haven't been given delivery dates for all my deepest wants, I do know all my aligned desires are meant for me and will arrive at the perfect time. I just have to manifest them.

The fastest way to do that is to drop the needy energy along the way.

TWENTY-SEVEN

BLOOD DIAMONDS

"I have standards I don't plan on lowering for anybody...including myself."
  —Zendaya

From: Maria E. Marcos
Sent: Thursday, February 18, 2016 11:07 AM
To: ISCU HelpDesk at Taylor St.
Subject: Katie Depaola CSOSA #:222501

To Whom It May Concern:
Please suspend the above referenced offender from further drug testing as she will now spot test according to minimum policy. Thank you for your assistance with this matter.

Sincerely,
Maria Marcos
Community Supervision Officer
Team #8

It was a Tuesday night and I was sitting in a tiny, stark white room with no windows and aged brown carpet that was frayed around the edges. Seven of us sat in a circle of dingy orange plastic chairs. The building was off Rhode Island Avenue in Northeast D.C.

How the hell did I get here? I asked myself.

I was a privileged, former Catholic schoolgirl who'd basically earned straight A's from kindergarten through high school graduation.

And yet there I was in a 22-week, court-mandated domestic violence intervention program. I did need an intervention.

It all started a few days after my nose job. Jesse was supposed to be taking care of me during my recovery. I had opened my computer to catch up on work, but Jesse didn't want me to work. His needs—sexual and otherwise—were *always* his top priority.

"If you can work, then you can take care of me," he said.

He pulled my computer from my hands. With post-op bandages still covering my nose, I wanted him to leave me alone. I stuck out my foot and flicked him away.

"Leave me alone," I said.

I didn't have much leverage. I was lying down, post-surgery, on the left side of my king-size bed, all five feet and four inches of me. He was standing all the way on the right. I could barely even reach him.

"I can't believe you just kicked your fiancé! I'm leaving," Jesse yelled like a child. He stormed his six-foot-four self out of my condo.

I hadn't kicked him, but I had kicked *at* him.

I should have let Jesse go right then. But 15 minutes after he left, I panicked. As I would learn in domestic violence class, I was smack in the middle of the cycle of abuse, which explained what happened next. He may have provoked me, but I was the one who apologized for something I never did.

I'm sorry for kicking you, I texted him. *Please come home.*

The bed was mine, just like the condo. I had made it. And now I had to lay in it.

I apologized for everything Jesse convinced me I had done wrong. Ironically, that text was what landed me in the program. It became evidence—and thank God for it, because like I said, I *needed* an intervention. The punishment may not have fit the crime, but I was there anyway, along with anywhere from three to 13 other women who came and went as they finished their 22 weeks. Mr. Collins was our facilitator and a licensed clinical professional counselor. The week I finished, he gave me a certificate of completion and said that even though I "lacked melanin," I'd done great. No one but me was white in the class, not even him, and he liked to tease me about that.

By the time I graduated, I'd grown to love Tuesday nights. Mr. Collins created a safe space for us to work out our issues. He was patient with us, often letting us process our anger out loud. There was always some shouting, a ton of laughter and a few tears. Eventually, he'd interrupt our banter and take the lead on settling the score. It was a different kind of camaraderie. Despite the varying experiences that had landed us there, we were bonded over something very real.

"I JUST MET him in passing, but he seems great," my friend said, and handed me a card. It was gold, made of plastic, and looked more like a credit card than a business card.

Jesse Jacobson, CEO and Rainmaker.

I'd just launched Whole Glow, was working full-time at the family business and had started my master's in nutrition. Fresh off a major breakup and sick with Lyme, I was a hot mess at the ripe age of 25. My friend thought I might benefit from meeting with a business coach.

Who would put "Rainmaker" on their business card? I rolled my eyes, went home and looked him up online. He had brown hair, a big smile and owned a jewelry business. He seemed successful—and maybe even cute.

The next morning, I called him. He asked me to come to his office and I did. He complimented my red lipstick and explained how we could work together. As he sketched out a diagram for my business, I was intrigued. He asked me to hire him as my business coach. I did.

At our second meeting, Jesse gave me a silver key necklace and said it was the key to my dreams. Jesse was married with two kids. He didn't hide that, but he also didn't hide his interest in me.

After we finished our coaching relationship, we stayed friends. Since I'd been his client, there was an implicit power dynamic. He knew everything about me—my challenges with my health, my stressors with work and school, my frustration with my brother Bo's ups and downs and, of course, my bad luck with dating. Once he decided to pursue me, he knew exactly how to do it. The situation escalated fast. I would never have pursued a married man, but he was extremely persistent. He said he hadn't been happy for years and was ready to leave his wife for me. According to

He's Just Not That Into You, wasn't Jesse's eagerness exactly what I was supposed to want?

When I say that my life was a disaster when Jesse came into it, I mean it was a complete disaster. In comparison to the rest of my unstable life, this shaky relationship felt somewhat secure. Jesse also showed up as a kind of savior, buying me gifts and confidently strategizing plans to take my business to the next level. As soon as I told him about my idea for Inner Glow Circle, he urged me to make it happen.

In the end, Jesse did leave his wife. He spent his first night alone in a hotel, then showed up at my condo the next day and never left. To say we were rushing things would be a drastic understatement. Within three months, I met his kids and became a bonus mom overnight. The kids were wonderful, but the relationship was not. I wanted partnership so badly that I ignored my intuition to run.

My brothers had taught me the importance of finding a lover and a protector in a partner, but there's a difference between protection and control—and between love and obsession.

———

WE GOT ENGAGED in December 2014. He gave me a ring, a Louis Vuitton suitcase and over-the-knee Louboutin boots. Then he told me he wanted 50 percent ownership of Inner Glow Circle. True partnership meant half and half, he said.

The following November, six months after Bo died and 11 months after I put that ring on my finger, I filed for a restraining order.

During those 11 months, we argued about everything. We fought about what I was wearing, where I was going and who I was with. When it came to business, we worked as a team, brainstorming, creating and coming up with new ideas. But our personal relationship was a catastrophe. The ring began to feel more like seven carats of hell than a symbol of love and commitment at all.

Jesse was over the top. When we had our worst fights, he would buy me bouquets that looked like they belonged in the lobby at the Four Seasons. I remember a friend saying I was so lucky. I told her, "The bigger the bouquet, the bigger the fight." My mom would ask, "What did he do to require that type of apology?"

He threatened to burn my clothes when I wore a dress he deemed too short. When he discovered I hadn't yet worn a pair of Jimmy Choo shoes he bought me, he threw them off the balcony. When we fought, Jesse would demand I give the ring back. A few times, he snatched it off my finger. During our very last fight, he pulled it so hard that he cut me. I watched my finger bleed and started making plans to leave.

As I had in the past, I stayed in a relationship that wasn't working, wasn't healthy and wasn't even close to what I wanted. Why? I was afraid to be alone. When Bo died, I became even more afraid. My depression brought me to rock bottom. It was less like, *I need someone to hang out with because I don't want to be alone* and more like, *I don't trust myself with myself right now.*

I didn't know the "kicking" episode would be our last official blowup. When Jesse walked out of the house and said he was leaving for what seemed like the gazillionth time, I knew he was bluffing. This was our game. Later that evening, Jesse came back. We made up, but on the inside, I had drifted to a new place.

A few nights later, Jesse went out with a friend and

stayed there. The next morning, I woke up to seven missed calls from him. When I called back, he was crying hysterically and said he was having thoughts of harming himself. He said if I really loved him, I would meet him at the ER.

On my way there, I tried to understand how things had escalated to that level. I couldn't figure out when or why he'd become so obsessive, controlling and narcissistic. Was it the stress of leaving his wife and kids? Was it the building financial pressure of the loans he owed on his business?

I found Jesse on a gurney in the hallway of the ER. "I'm not okay," he said. His face was pink, his eyes bloodshot. He couldn't stop crying.

"I understand." I put my hand on his shoulder. I was acting compassionate, but I was exhausted and annoyed. It had been almost a year of fighting and drama, and it wasn't the first time we'd come to the hospital because Jesse "wasn't feeling right." I caught a few words—psychiatrist, tests, transfer—from the swarm of nurses talking nearby, but was promptly ushered out. Eventually, someone told me he was being taken to the Psychiatric Institute.

"Take my phone," Jesse said, handing it to me. "Business as usual. Don't tell anyone I'm here."

"Got it," I said. *As if I want anyone to know I'm living in a complete and total nightmare*, I thought.

The next 24 hours were an insane blur. My energy levels were totally tanked, but I had a podcast recording on the schedule. When I finished with the interview, there were five missed calls on my phone from an unknown local number.

The voicemail was crackly and distressed. "Your fiancé is in the psych ward and you're not even picking up. I can't believe you're doing this to me."

It was Jesse. His second voicemail was punctuated with

long pauses. "Call me back." He gave me the number. "When you call, say 'code blue' and they'll know where to transfer you."

I followed his instructions. I was still his puppet.

"I'm looking to speak with Jesse Jacobson," I said. "He told me to call and say, 'code blue.'"

The person on the other end of the line connected me to Jesse. He said he was using a phone booth in the hallway, he was doing great, everyone was so impressed with him and they were going to let him out soon. I asked him if he thought it might be good for him to stay a bit longer.

"I need to get out of here," he said.

Another night went by. I woke up to a new voicemail. "Just so you know, Katie, this is over. We're over. We're not engaged anymore. I hope you understand that."

My entire body relaxed. I felt relieved.

But relieved or not, what happened next looked more like a dysfunctional divorce than a typical breakup. Within a week, I filed a protective order against Jesse for stalking. He wouldn't leave me alone.

My false apology for the "kicking" allowed him to retaliate and file a protective order against me in return. It also landed me in the domestic violence class. All of a sudden, "Miss Straight A's" had weekly drug tests, occasional home visits and a probation officer.

Even though it sucked to get accused of something I didn't do, mutual restraining orders were the best thing that could have happened between me and Jesse. We were so addicted to our cycle that we needed the space only a court order could create. We needed it to be illegal for us to communicate. It was the only way to break up that level of codependency.

The entire split—including court dates and regaining

full ownership of my company—took nearly a year. By the time it was over, I was emotionally, physically and financially drained.

It was an out-of-body experience to watch my dad testify against my ex-fiancé and to represent myself in court, which, although I don't advise it, was what I decided to do. My family always said I should be an attorney, but this courtroom scene wasn't what they'd had in mind. They hadn't seen the domestic violence class coming, either.

———

"WHO CAN EXPLAIN the cycle of abuse to the rest of the class?" Mr. Collins would say. This was our moment to admit how we had participated in the harmful cycle of our relationships. Most of us *had* engaged in some way. We'd gotten into these situations because there was something inside of us that wanted to fight back. We stayed because we couldn't just walk away.

Once I learned about the cycle of abuse—which starts with tension-building, leads to explosion and ends with the honeymoon stage—I got it. In the beginning, the arguments, name-calling and manipulation were all-consuming. They always escalated to a dramatic blowup, with tears, anger and violent behavior. But then, with the release of pressure, the honeymoon phase would start again. Profuse apologies, over-the-top gestures, expensive gifts and obsessive attention were how Jesse attempted to erase the trauma. It was pure psychological abuse. He was unwell—and so was I.

In the domestic violence program, I also learned how privileged I was to have gotten out of my situation. It shocked me how many women in the group were still in relationships with the people who'd gotten them there.

Apparently, you *can* still live with someone while they have a restraining order against you. It's just a game of cat and mouse to see if the person who filed the order reports a violation. Like me, most of the women were not the perpetrators in their relationships. One woman threw her husband's cell phone when she found him cheating and he got an order against her. Another scratched her husband when she caught him doing drugs with their son, and she was the one sent to the program. The system doesn't protect women—and it certainly doesn't protect Black women or women of color.

I can't say the program changed me into a woman who walks away. It took far more than 22 weeks to have that breakthrough, but it did teach me to never again put someone else's well-being above my own sanity and peace of mind, regardless of how afraid I was to be alone. It also taught me not to apologize for things I didn't do.

I completed my time in the program on August 23, 2016. I know the date because I have a picture of my graduation certificate signed by Mr. Collins.

By the time I graduated, I'd already gotten rid of everything that reminded me of Jesse—anything he bought me, any furniture he sat on, anything he'd touched. I sold it, trashed it or gave it away. His energy was so enmeshed with mine that I couldn't shake him off easily. I had to get rid of everything to get rid of him.

Keeping the certificate itself felt unnecessary and honestly retraumatizing, but I did take a photo. In it, I'm sitting in the backseat of my dad's car on the day my parents picked me up from my final class. I didn't have driving limitations, but my dad and I had a routine. He would leave work, pick me up at my condo in Northwest D.C., drop me off at class in Northeast and answer emails on his phone until it was time to go home. I think it was his way of trying to help bear my burden. It was an unexpected bonding experience, and further evidence of my privilege.

I never wanted to be defined by my white privilege, and in this case, my whiteness hadn't saved me from the system. But my privileges were still glaring.

I was white and I had no choice but to look at my whiteness. Some of the deepest anti-racism work I've ever done happened in that program.

Week after week, I showed up in a black leather baseball cap and black leggings with a black Valentino bag. I kept my head down and listened. I learned about the obvious and more nuanced ways my life was different, even though we were sitting in the same classroom. When I say I got close with the other women, I mean we got close. We became friends on Facebook, exchanged phone numbers and checked in on each other between classes. But it wasn't lost on me that my dad was outside waiting for me in a Mercedes, while the majority were taking the bus home alone—and often still living with their abuser.

On the final day of class, both of my parents were there to pick me up. When I got in the car, smiling with relief and holding my certificate, there was a bouquet of flowers and a card on the seat. They were proud of me for humbly "doing my time."

I get how weird it all is, but it's also my life, my truth-truth.

"Have you learned to be careful about what you put in writing?" my mom asked.

My parents were overly supportive. After losing a child less than a year before, they didn't judge me. They just wanted to be by my side. Plus, they'd never wanted me to end up with Jesse. They never trusted him or the fast pace of our relationship.

Sometimes, people ask me why I stayed with Jesse for so long. My only answer is this: I stayed as long as I did so I could tell you about it. One day longer and I don't know if I'd be alive—seriously. Whether it's a big ring or gushy social media posts, what looks good on the outside is sometimes very, very bad. It's humiliating to look back at what I put myself through, but it's a dark reality for so many people.

At the end of the day—and at the end of a relationship—ownership is everything. It's how you take charge and find your power again. It's how you say, "You know what? This *did* happen and it was terrible, but now I'm okay." And then you say to yourself, to the world, to the ex who tried to take everything, "I'm going to make something out of this. I'm going to rise up and find the glow in the dark. I'm going to glow through what I go through."

Crazy situations, unhealthy relationships and business ups and downs can feel exhilarating at times. Who knows what's going to happen next? But crazy is fun until crazy gets old. And for me, it did. Eventually, I got bored of my own drama. I got bored of dating the same flavors of unhealthy men over and over again. Most of all, I got bored of my own excuses.

I couldn't change my entire life overnight, but I *could* change my mindset. That's when I decided to not only find the glow in the dark, but to *become* it. I wasn't just going to *survive* the fallout with Jesse. I was going to rise from the ashes, bigger and braver than ever before.

Finding the good in a bad situation does not mean you immediately jet off into bliss. It's not about denial. It's about transformation. It's about evolution. You take what you've been through, accept it as truth and decide to make it into something new.

"YOU'RE GOING to make millions from this," Joe said.

In order to untangle my life from Jesse's, I had to hire a few lawyers. Joe was my favorite. He had a jolly, matter-of-fact presence. I know you're not necessarily supposed to trust lawyers, but I trusted Joe. This is what he said to me one day when I broke into tears on the phone.

"You really think I'll make millions?" I asked. "How?"

"A TV show? A book? I don't know, but don't worry about everything so much."

When it came time for Jesse to sign the papers and release his 50 percent ownership of my company, it was—surprisingly—the new woman in his life who saved the day. Less than a year after our breakup, Jesse was engaged again, and as it turned out, his new fiancée was also his attorney. At first, I was hurt that he'd wrangled his new woman to represent him in the case against his last one. But in the end, her involvement saved the day.

My guess is that she wanted him all to herself and any attachment to another woman wasn't good for her. The papers were prepared and she told Joe that Jesse would be signing them over the weekend. Monday came and the papers sat, unsigned. I wondered what was going on. A few days later, Jesse posted on social media that he was single again. He was always quick to publicize his private news.

I felt defeated. We had almost reached the finish line. Joe urged me to be patient and said the situation would ulti-mately work in our favor. He was right. Jesse got back with his attorney-slash-fiancée and a few days later, I received a signed copy of the reassignment agreement in my inbox.

I paid Jesse one freaking dollar for full ownership of Inner Glow Circle. After nearly a year of fighting in court and a painful $20,000 in legal fees, I was free.

———

WHEN YOU LOSE SO MUCH SO QUICKLY, it can feel like your free will has been taken away. Your sense of hope is gone faster than words written in the sand, wiped out by the rising tide. You may feel like a victim because you are one. If you want to, you can keep *choosing* victim. That identity might even become comfortable for you. It became comfortable for me.

Eventually, the victim identity didn't fit for me anymore. I wanted to step fully into the role of victor.

When I was in the thick of some of my toughest times, my dad sent me a series of texts that gave me the confidence I needed to forge ahead. They relit my inner fire so I could keep glowing through what I was going through. Now, I pass them on to you.

Texts from my dad: *A powerful woman doesn't need anyone else to complete her mission to change the world. I know you are in pain right now, but God is throwing a big challenge your way to test your mettle, to really see what you're made of. He is testing your commitment to other women right now.*

It is in times like these that we find our true selves. I had plenty of times when the deck was stacked against me, when banks were calling and wanted to take our lines of credit, when I wondered what was going to happen next with the

company. I hid these challenges from you and Mom. I perse-
vered and it paid off.

You may not know why but you will find out soon what
the reason for this is and it will pay off huge for you. I have
always believed in you!!! You are someone very special and
your calling is to make your mark on the world and help
other women.

TWENTY-EIGHT

THE END OF AN ERA

"If death meant just leaving the stage long enough to change costume and come back as a new character, would you slow down? Or speed up?"
—Chuck Palahniuk

"Bo's dead. You need to come home." Johnny's voice was steady and matter-of-fact.

I was staying at the Ritz-Carlton in San Francisco when I got the news. I was in that half-asleep-not-fully-oriented-to-my-surroundings state when I answered Johnny's call.

I remember picking up a few issues of *Vogue* from one of the hotel tables and throwing them at the perfectly wall-papered walls of the Ritz. I remember screaming at the top of my lungs.

I don't remember much after that.

For what it's worth, I find a lot of peace in knowing Bo lived a really great life. We traveled a lot as kids. We went to Costa Rica, Mexico, Australia and Italy. We went to the beach every summer and skiing every winter. We were spoiled and well-loved.

Our last family trip with Bo was to Puerto Rico. We visited a bioluminescent bay, a rare ecosystem filled with microscopic organisms that glow when they're disturbed. Because there are millions of these organisms in the bay, when you paddle or splash around, they light up in a neon blue-green color and create a glow in the dark effect.

I had the most otherworldly experience kayaking that night. I looked up and saw a full spectrum grid spread out across the dark night sky. It looked like a thin, glowing, light blue web. In the corners of the grids were what I can only describe as angelic figures. They didn't look like specific people, but more like illuminated energies floating and hovering overhead. They had wings.

It wasn't a drug-induced experience, but it felt totally trippy. I blinked my eyes repeatedly to make sure what I was seeing was really there. To date, it was the most euphoric experience of my life.

Bo and I were in the same kayak the night I saw this angelic grid in the sky. I'll never know whether he also saw it, but if he did, maybe he took it as his invitation to go home.

Even in the midst of beautiful experiences like a vacation to Puerto Rico, Bo was struggling. It's hard to say which behaviors were caused by drugs, which were evidence of an issue with his mental health and which could simply be attributed to the typical challenges of being a teenager. Co-occurring diagnoses often compound the confusion in understanding and treating mental health and addiction.

AS SOON AS Johnny told me that Bo had died, I heard two words in my mind: "It's done." It was like my life was being narrated. A major chapter had ended, and it was the worst ending I could have imagined. As I waited for the concierge to help me find a flight home, I sat in the bathtub at the Ritz, ran hot water over my feet and put my head between my knees. Then I called my psychic.

"Oh my stars," Karen said over and over again. Then she told me that Bo had been scooped up by two other angels, both family members. She said he was at peace when he passed and that he wasn't in any pain.

On the way home from San Francisco, a lady in the airport saw me sobbing and asked me what had happened. How do you tell a stranger in the airport that your brother just died? I somehow did. She ran to the snack kiosk and bought me chocolate-covered blueberries. I didn't ask her for them, but what else do you do when a stranger tells you she's traveling home because her brother just died?

When I finally got to my parents' house, we lit candles and prayed. My friends came and gathered. My cousins held me as I cried. I heard my mother grieve. I watched my dad break down. I'd tell you more details, but honestly, I don't remember much. I just felt like a part of me had died. It was a dark and hopeless time. I felt everything and nothing.

The Catholic tradition is to hold viewings with an open casket. Those final moments were tragic, but he looked damn good. Even lying in his casket, Bo was handsome. As a kid, he had a giant smile and big dimples. When he passed, he was still smiling. His death made me more certain than ever that there's peace on the other side.

I kneeled by my brother's casket, held his hand and talked to him. I was surprised by how comfortable I felt being close to him, because dead people had always freaked me out. I'm down with angels and shit, but dead bodies? No thank you. But Bo wasn't a body. He was my brother, my family, a piece of me. I'd changed his diapers, kissed him, held him and yelled at him for playing tricks on me. As I held his hand this last time, I told him that I loved him and that I would miss him so much. It felt so finite.

When the funeral director said it was time to close the casket, I kissed Bo on the forehead as I'd done so many times. He was cold. It felt wrong to leave him there. My parents, Johnny and I kneeled together. My mom had been so poised all day. Even at this major low, my parents were kind and gracious. As they closed the casket, I heard a sound from my mom that still rings in my ears. It was the sound of a mother losing her child. I wrapped my arms around her as we got up to leave.

"Do you think he's going to be okay by himself?" my dad whispered in my ear as we walked out of the funeral home, sniffling and trying to maintain his composure.

"I think he'll be okay," I said.

What I didn't know was whether I'd be okay. Would any of us ever be okay again?

TWENTY-NINE

HE'S NOT DEAD

"Knowing what must be done does away with fear."
—Rosa Parks

The next day, we held a Mass. My brother's funeral was the most mind-altering experience of my life. It was all happening around me, but none of it added up.

My family stood in the hallway of the church, greeting the people who came to pay their respects. We have a family business, so we know how to be professional. We can do things like show up and say hello, even when it hurts, even when it's hard.

My dad and I gave eulogies. During mine, I shared my memories of Bo and read a poem I'd written for him.

Come Back to Me

Goodbye, sweet child,
May you fly on angels' wings

Learn what you need to learn,
Be who you need to be.
And then, when your work is done
And you've passed the tests of heaven,
Come back to us.
When you've seen
And really felt
How loved you are,
How perfect you are,
In every way,
Come back here, you beautiful boy.
Come back to me.

The poem was laced with messages of reincarnation, and I felt rebellious reading it out loud in a Catholic church. Still, it was discreet enough to feel like a secret only Bo and I knew. I held on to that. Days before the Mass, back in San Francisco, when I'd been sitting alone in the bathtub trying to process what had happened, I'd had a radical thought. It was more like a sense of knowing. *He's going to come back to me. He's going to come back in this lifetime.* My poem was a recognition of this, but it was also a direct message to my brother.

You better come back here, Bo.

Once, long before Bo passed, I asked Karen what happens when people die. She told me that every death is ultimately a suicide. "We are all born with exit dates, dates we can choose to leave this place if it gets too hard," she said. "If someone chooses an exit date before they've learned all their karmic lessons, they'll get reborn into the same family or a similar one."

I don't know if this is the full truth, but the way Karen said it made it sound very real. Maybe Bo didn't learn all his lessons in this lifetime and maybe he would be coming back. I hoped he would.

At the end of the service, Johnny gathered with a bunch of our cousins around the casket. They were wearing Bo's favorite hats, preparing to carry the casket out to the hearse. We drove up the road to the cemetery. We walked up to the seven plots that my grandma had, by chance, purchased for our family two months earlier. When she bought them, she'd been thinking of herself and Grandad, not Bo.

The priest said his final words, the casket was lowered and I watched my grandad cry. All at once, Johnny and our cousins threw Bo's hats deep into the grave so he would be surrounded by things he loved. As if on command, a swarm of orange butterflies flew through the tent where we were gathered. Everyone noticed. Everyone was in awe.

FOR A LONG TIME, I walked around with a song of grief repeating in my head. *My brother is gone. I've lost everything. I'll never be the same.*

I imprinted these thoughts in my mind and tattooed visuals of them on my body. I talked about them online, to my friends and to my many therapists.

One day, I was running through my usual list: *My brother is gone. I've lost everything. I'll never be the same.* I'd gotten comfortable living with these words on repeat. But this time, something different happened. I'd been thinking the same thoughts for almost two years, and all of a sudden, I heard a different response. Maybe it was from God or maybe it was from some future version of myself. *What if he's not dead?*

It stopped me in my tracks. *Now that's a radical, radical thought.*

I know from my work as a coach that when you're stuck in a repeating pattern, sometimes the only thing you need is to choose a new one. Somehow, this new thought had chosen me. It was another download that had landed in my brain, seemingly out of nowhere.

Was it true that Bo was dead? Yes. Was it *really* true? I wasn't sure.

Literally speaking, I believed the old thought. I remembered that his skin felt cold on my lips when I finally got the guts to kiss him goodbye before they closed the casket. I remembered watching the casket as it was lowered into the ground.

But I also believed the new thought. In fact, I had *proof* he was still alive. We started communicating pretty soon after he passed and our talks had become routine. I could sense where he was standing in my room and I could feel him sitting with me in the car. I could tell when he would mess with the order of songs on my playlist. I could even hear his laugh when Johnny and I mentioned his name. When we'd joke about him, I could hear his familiar voice telling us to lay off. Throughout the Christmas season and around his birthday, he sent Amazon boxes with his name on them to my parents' house and to mine. They said Bo. It was always a zero at the end instead of an "O," but I'm not one to nitpick signs from the other side.

ONE DAY, I started to ask myself: *What have I gained from all this loss? What if these losses were actually gifts?*

The end of my relationship had clearly been a blessing,

but it was hard to find any gratitude in being sick for over a decade. And when it came to my brother, I knew it would be beyond radical to truly celebrate a loss of that magnitude. I knew I would be criticized and that many people wouldn't be ready for my approach. I knew it could be too fast, even for me. But something inside me said looking at things from the perspective that Bo might *actually* still be alive was the only way for me to keep living.

So, I made a life-changing choice. I decided to celebrate all of it. I wanted to not only celebrate that he had lived, but also that he had died and was now living in a whole new way. It's not common and it's not traditional, but I decided I was going to stop listening to the people who said the grief would never go away. I had to buy into my own radical perspective.

———

A FEW MONTHS after Bo died, I wrote him a letter. Karen told me he was asking to hear from me, so I followed her directions. While I typed, Bo started talking back to me.

August 15, 2015

Dear Bo,

I miss you completely. Like, my whole heart misses you. It's a weird experience to lose your brother forever. I remember losing you in the grocery store when you were two years old, rambunctious as hell and refusing to slow down for anyone. I was terrified then. Now, I'm frozen.

My heart is hurting more than I can put into words. Life has continued on. Businesses and families are growing, but grief has darkened things. "It's only made the dark things darker," I hear you whisper to me as I write this letter, the letter you asked me to write.

I'm not mad at you. I really do understand. A part of me has wanted to leave since I came here, but life is rich, continues to teach me and keeps me here, feet firmly on the ground. No matter how often I float up into the sky, I always come back. Earth is my place for this lifetime. That is one thing I'm beginning to accept.

My psychic Karen was pretty adamant about you wanting me to write this letter. And she was pretty clear that I actually am mad at you.

"If you're not mad, why are you yelling when you're alone in the house?"

Well, then. I didn't know you saw that, but thanks for asking. You were always clear and direct, even amidst your unconcerned ways.

I'm mad you hurt Mom. I'm mad Dad spent so much time and energy on you. I felt forgotten a lot of the time, even though I knew you were sick. I'm sick too, ya know. I finally figured out what's wrong on my own, but it hasn't been easy, buddy.

I know you didn't leave on purpose in the world's eyes, but I believe every soul ultimately makes its own choices. If this was your time to go, I trust that. I trust that you knew, but it doesn't make it any easier. There are so many people here who are still grieving, who still don't understand your journey or why you left when you did.

I know I am not alone in my grief. I feel you by my side, wrapping your angel arms around me. I sense your presence in the moments I actually stop to pay attention. I even smelled your cologne when I was writing about you the other night. That's how I know you're around.

You died in your sleep. How peaceful. How beautiful. How tragic.

Sometimes I get so sad we weren't closer when you were here. But now I understand why you had your walls up. You didn't want to hurt us any more than you had to.

I love you, buddy. I respect you for your journey here on this planet. I'm grateful for the change you've inspired in all of us. I love you for who you are, not who you weren't, and ultimately, I'm eager to have a different kind of relationship with you.

Just as I'm closing out this letter, of course you send me a flash of a memory. It's a quote from that Robert Munsch book I used to read to you when you were little.

"I'll love you forever, I'll like you for always, as long as I'm living my baby you'll be."

I'll keep living. You go ahead and rest in peace.

Love,
Your big sis

IF YOU WANT to fall in love with losing like I did, you have to be open to taking a new approach to your grief. You have to be willing to write letters that may never be read and, most importantly, to question everything. You have to be willing to see the glow in the dark for every situation.

The glow in the dark is more than the silver lining. It's the thing to get excited about before it even happens, before you're ready, before you want to. The glow in the dark is the opportunity on the other side of the pain—and finding it is the only way we will survive this wild and crazy life.

THIRTY

COME BACK TO ME

"The past is over and done and cannot be changed. This is the only moment we can experience. Deep at the center of my being there is an infinite well of gratitude."

—Louise Hay

Soon after I started to shift my mindset around loss, things did start coming back to me. In May 2017, after five years apart, PJ was back.

Have you heard of "meet cutes?" They're most common in rom-coms, when two romantic leads cross paths for the first time in a way-too-cute-to-be-real sort of way. No one meets like that in real life. These days, everyone meets online.

When PJ and I met again, it couldn't have been a meet cute, because we'd already met. We'd been through some shit in our years together, and even more individually in the years we'd been apart. The timing of our reconnection was bizarre. It was two months after I completed my partial hospitalization program. I'd just come to terms with the extent of my PTSD and had started treatment with the Lyme doctor who would eventually cure me. A lot of healing was happening in my world.

Because of this, I like to think of my reconnection with PJ as a "meet spiritual." The actual date of our meet spiritual was even weirder. It was the two-year anniversary of losing Bo.

The time lapse of two years felt significant to me. When Bo passed, a friend who'd lost her dad told me it had taken her two years to feel like herself again. When I heard that, I promised I would give myself the same amount of time to heal. And I did. I grieved hard for two years.

As I neared the two-year mark, the pressure to get my shit together grew. I asked Bo for help. I asked him to teach me how to live and how to glow through what I was going through. I asked him to show me how to celebrate his life, death and whatever afterlife he was in. I asked him to help me open to love again.

That's when PJ showed up—both familiar and evolved, both old and new.

SITTING at a fancy rooftop pool in San Antonio, a year into our reunion, I gazed across the water at the man who used to be mine all those years ago. He had come back to me. I thought of my brother and the poem I wrote when he passed, the one I read at his funeral. Without knowing it, maybe some part of it was for PJ, too.

I noticed how the sun glistened off PJ's body as he swam. The water seemed to sparkle around him. My hair was blonder than ever and I hoped the sun would lighten it even more. It was obvious I'd gone to lengths to lighten things up, hoping that lightening things on the outside would somehow translate to the inside. I thought about the beautiful home I'd created back in D.C., the company I was slowly but surely building and the core relationships I had invested in and worked hard to maintain.

Life is hard, but good, I thought. *I created this.*

A butterfly landed on my arm. I stayed quiet, trying my best to keep him there.

This is a sign, I whispered to myself. *I am alive. I've gotten hold of my mind and a new life has followed.*

I believe in reincarnation because I believe in second chances. I also know you can be reborn in *this* lifetime. I know because it happened to me. I was reborn. It wasn't an easy journey, but all my effort was finally starting to feel like it was worth something. Miracles were coming to me.

I took a breath and paused to check my phone. As I pressed the button on the side, the screen lit up with the time: 5:23 pm.

Of course, I thought. *Bo died on May 23 and he's been showing me those numbers ever since.*

On that rooftop in San Antonio with PJ, I smiled, realizing it also happened to be the day before what would have been Bo's 23rd birthday.

A few months later, PJ and I were in New York City for the weekend. I asked if we could walk by our old work building, where we'd met eight years earlier. When we got there, I couldn't believe my eyes. I knew the office had been on East 23rd Street, but I didn't remember it was 50 East 23rd Street. There it was again: 523.

To me, experiencing these signs *with* PJ meant we were supposed to be together, especially since he'd known my brother all those years ago. I took the signs seriously, because PJ's preexisting relationship with my entire family —and especially with Bo—made me feel like he was connected to something essential about my past.

The relationship was full of ups and downs. Over the course of the two and a half years after our meet spiritual, we had many labels. We were friends, more than friends, friends with benefits, unofficially dating, committed but not in a relationship and eventually—when we both got tired enough—in a relationship. A few days after we made things official, PJ moved in. A month after that, he moved out.

I fought hard for our love. I fought hard for the shred of hope that told me being with PJ might somehow keep me connected with Bo. I was still a fighter. I hadn't learned how to walk away.

THROUGHOUT MY FIGHT, PJ was unfailingly honest. He loved me, he didn't want to lose me and he was facing his own internal battle. He needed to deal with the void inside himself. I believed him when he said that. I never thought that he just wasn't that into me. I knew he was healing his own patterns. Since I was doing the same, I couldn't judge.

I solidified two more dating rules during round two with PJ.

The first rule is that when you want a relationship to work, you must practice the art of being all in.

You love who you love, and when it comes to raw feelings, you might not always have a choice in the matter. Relationships, though, are ultimately something you choose. For a partnership to work, you must *choose* it. You must take a stand for the partnership and go all in. You can't show up one way when you're dating and magically expect things to evolve as you get more serious. Relationships evolve as *we* evolve them. The only way to give a relationship a real shot is to commit to being fully in it and show up as your authentic self at every stage.

I loved PJ, so I listened to him. I gave him space. I knew if I was attracting a certain experience (in this case, his lack of commitment), there was something in me that felt comfortable there, even if I said I didn't want it. It seemed like the right time to take another look at myself. One particular pattern of mine came to light. Because PJ wasn't fully committing, I was keeping a few things running on the side.

In essence, I was still working the Four Man Plan.

You already know that if there was a game to be played, I was going to play it. But for the first time in a while, I started asking myself some big questions about my strategy. *Why do I keep other men on backup? Why do I pull out my phone to text someone else the moment PJ is unavailable? Why am I afraid to be alone?*

I decided to change these behaviors once and for all. If I wanted a committed relationship, I had to play all in myself even if the other person wasn't there yet. Although it destroyed the remaining bits of my ego, I called the other guys and told them I was seeing someone and needed to give that a real chance. I would make PJ my three-and-a-half man and see what happened.

As it turned out, I had to simplify things to get to the root of my issues and face my fear of being alone. Investing in my relationship with PJ and understanding what parts of me weren't actually aligned with a committed relationship —like the parts that were constantly texting other men—

ultimately brought me back to myself. I had to figure out why I needed so much attention to begin with.

The second rule I added to my list was this: You should stay in a relationship as long as you're still learning.

Relationships are teachers meant to evolve you into the next version of yourself. Most of us strive for perfection, but the point of relationships is practice. Since the main function of a relationship is your own personal growth, as long as you're still learning, you're on the right path. Dating, intimacy and partnership require massive trust in yourself, in your partner and in the universe.

The flip side of this rule is that as soon as you stop growing, it's time to go.

I interpreted so many external occurrences as signs that I should be with PJ. But what it ultimately boiled down to was that I was looking outside of myself for direction instead of trusting my intuition. The relationship became difficult and I felt like I was holding it together for both of us in an unhealthy way. Even though PJ had come back to me, I couldn't be attached to the idea of him staying forever.

Still, round two with PJ was proof that people could come back—and that in and of itself was important. PJ had evolved and so had I.

Strangely, as my life got better, PJ started to pull back. When my brother, Johnny, married my sister-in-law, Thabata, and they had their son, PJ became painfully disconnected. But then a miracle happened.

As I felt PJ pulling away, Bo's energy started coming back to me.

We found out about my nephew the night before Grandad passed, which was a magical reminder of the circle of life, The Cycle of Loving and Losing. Overnight, our family lost one life and gained another.

I felt Grandad and Bo working together from the other side, Grandad making way for Johnny's new baby and Bo's energy coming back through him, the cycle continuing to flow through all of our lives. As new life came into my world, the love I had been working for started to fade away.

I'd always loved being single, so I couldn't figure out why I was fearing it as things went south with PJ. Hadn't I had some of the most exciting times of my life when I was single, studying abroad in Australia and living in New York City in my early 20s? I took a good look at my actual experiences as an unattached woman and asked myself what stories I was telling myself around regaining my single status.

Once again, I discovered that I'd developed a limiting belief. The story on repeat this time was, *If I'm single, I'm not worthy.* I was just shy of 32 but operating from my 14-year-old fears.

I adopted a new thought: *My relationship status has nothing to do with my worth.*

There was one more thing I had to do before I could move forward. I imagined visiting my 14-year-old self during the breakup with Kyle. I imagined sitting by her side, holding her hand as she cried on her dad's shoulder during her first and most impactful breakup. I owed her that.

We're all afraid to lose things we love. But the fear of loss is just a lack of belief that something greater exists. It was time to fine-tune my energy. I had to set boundaries around what was and wasn't going to work in my life. As soon as I did that, things shifted completely.

EVERY TIME I went through a breakup, my dad said the same thing. "This is great, Katie!"

Then he would tell me that if I was single, I was *finally* available for the right man to come along. The right relationships always get better and getting rid of a relationship that's wrong is never a bad move. What's tough is knowing when to leave.

Recently, I was talking to a close friend who's dating an unavailable man. He might be available in the future, but he's not right now.

"If there was someone greater for you, would you want him?" I asked her.

"No, I just want *him*," she said, referring to the unavailable man. This surprised me.

We talked through my question further, and I shared that even though I'm currently experiencing great love with a man who *is* available, if there is a greater love for me in this lifetime, I want the one that's greater. My friend understood what I was saying, but that didn't change her pain. She was still caught up in questions that had no answers. *Why couldn't the unavailable man become available right now?*

Instead of accepting what life is showing us, we get all existential about it. We want to understand why. *Why did I meet them if I couldn't have them fully? Why am I going through this? What is this person's purpose in my life?* Maybe this person showed up to make you stronger or more humble. Maybe they're meant to teach you fun and adventure. Maybe they're here to be a mirror and show you more of who you are.

Love is a great teacher and sometimes it's impossible to fully grasp the reason behind each experience. Every connection is a divine lesson. Each relationship opens you further.

A potential partner may pull you in and then push you away, leaving you confused. In this case, they are refusing to do the complete work to make themselves available to you. This lack of availability might show up as resistance to working through physical or emotional distance, an attachment to a previous relationship, an unwillingness to let go of dating others or an inability to focus on anything other than their own healing or recovery. These may be healthy choices for your partner. But what's healthy for your partner isn't necessarily healthy for you.

If a dating dynamic feels off and you sense you're being guided another way, don't resist the redirection.

Consider these reasons a potential partner may choose not to rise to the occasion in a relationship:

1. They do not know how to love you because they do not yet fully love themselves.
2. You are healed and they are still healing.
3. They are healed and you are still healing.
4. They do not know if they can make you happy.
5. They know on a soul level that there is a greater match coming for you.

In my case, I eventually realized it was time to grow and glow. Before PJ and I had even made the final decision to part ways, I went back to the manifestation drawing board. I had to get clear on exactly what I wanted and start attracting it into my life. This time, though, I wasn't just manifesting a husband. I'd almost *had* a husband. There had even been a proposal and a ring—and we all know how that ended.

A husband wasn't my Greatest Level of Want. My G.L.O.W. was to find my soulmate, the partner who embodied everything I deserved. As I started doing this work, I kept an open mind that PJ could still be my soulmate, but I also opened to the idea of someone new. When you're manifesting, you can't get attached to any single outcome. You have to stay open to "this or something better."

I started to make a list of everything I desired in a partner. I wrote down the best qualities I'd seen in everyone I'd ever dated and let myself believe there was one person who would embody them all.

I want someone who's awake.
An awakened partnership, a pure love.
Lots of spaciousness, freedom and mutual respect.
Immense trust and "coming home" to one another and the partnership.
I want full support of each other's dreams and desires.
I want someone who does the work, who is energetically and emotionally responsible.
I want someone who is my partner, who challenges me, protects us and is a safe place to land.
I want someone who is loyal, forgiving of themself, me and the world.
I want someone who is activated and whose presence is activating to me.

Halfway through, I shifted from what I wanted to what I deserved.

I deserve a partner who I can trust, who has healthy boundaries.

I deserve a partner who shows up for me and for us.
I deserve a partner who is honest and who I can be honest with too.
I deserve a partner who gives me space to work, to create, to be me.
I deserve a partner who encourages me to read, learn and grow and who does the same.
I deserve a partner who can own their part in the equation and who is willing to make amends.
I deserve a partner who wants a strong woman, who has never met anyone like me and who is inspired and motivated by my focus, passion and drive.

Done, I looked at this list and did a review of myself. Was there anything listed that I wasn't being, that I was asking for in someone else, but hadn't explored in my own evolution? It was the most powerful integrity check. If I wanted an honest partner, I had to be honest. If I wanted someone who was settled into their life, I had to settle into mine. If I wanted someone powerful, I had to be powerful too. I made a commitment to become what I desired and felt my energy expand.

When a partner is living in your home, the breakup takes longer than it otherwise would. And often, that's where the healing happens. Through conversations we had while moving boxes out of my house, PJ and I did what we could to get closure together. The rest was up to me.

I continued manifesting my soulmate and staying open to my own evolution. In the weeks after our breakup, I meditated almost every day and imagined what it would feel like to lay in my future partner's arms. I didn't imagine PJ or any other person in particular. I just imagined the feeling I would have when I was with this person.

All I knew was it felt good.

I was sad about PJ and I missed the time we'd spent together, but as I moved through the heartbreak, I kept asking myself what opportunity there might be in this experience. If you want to glow in the dark, you must have a radical commitment to seeing everything in your life as an opportunity. No matter what happens, no matter what challenges you face, you must explore the potential opportunities—even in sickness, even in loss and even in great tragedy.

This is not the Law of Attraction, because you aren't attracting. It's the Law of *Creation*, where you look at what actually *is* and create beauty from there.

Before you're ready (while keeping in mind that "ready" is a lie), your prayer becomes, *God, show me the opportunity here. Let me transmute this. Let me use this for good.*

According to the Law of Equal Exchange, for everything gained, something equal is lost. And for everything lost, something equal is gained. Nothing ever really gets created or destroyed. It simply changes form.

It's not easy to let go, to be free or to open yourself to what's on the other side of life's most painful experiences. Moving through loss will be the most difficult experience of your life, but it will also give you *back* your life. You will live again in a whole new way. Every time you love and lose, it's like a death. When you feel strong enough and when you choose to, you get reborn into something new. Your pain becomes your magic, your inspiration, your spark. You become the glow in the dark.

You can trust yourself to go into the darkness, even if you're afraid. Again and again, you will be liberated by your light.

THIRTY-ONE

MAKING LOVE

"I have learned not to worry about love, but to honor its coming with all my heart."
—Alice Walker

I'm sitting on a king-size bed at the Four Seasons hotel in downtown Manhattan. I'm wearing light blue pajamas and I'm surrounded by eight oversized down pillows. To call it luxury would be an understatement.

I'm on the phone with Gram, who's telling me that my brother, Johnny, is having breathing problems and is about to be transferred to the ICU. She says I should consider catching a train home tomorrow, especially since my parents are still in Paris. I'm nervous, but I'm grateful that I'm not alone. Adam is here.

He's sitting next to me watching a late-night talk show. The second I hang up the phone, he puts his hand on my leg. "Are you okay?"

"I'm nervous," I tell him. "I've been here before."

"I know," he says. "It sounds bad. What do you want to do?"

"I don't like being away from home, but I don't want to leave you yet, either."

"I understand that. Come here." He reaches for my hand, pulls me close and puts his arm around me. I'm wrapped up in him. I can't believe we've been friends for all these years and now he's the one holding my hand.

Life is so weird. You never know where love is going to take you next.

It's been four and a half years since we lost Bo, and I really *have* healed. But the PTSD hasn't gone away completely. I still experience triggers from certain situations that feel familiar, similar to past traumas. My mind flashes back to the last time I was in a fancy hotel room on a similar call. That time, it had been Johnny calling about Bo.

Why am I always away from home when this shit happens? I ask myself. *I can't possibly be losing another brother. That can't be how this story goes. God wouldn't let that happen to me. I already told Her I'm done with the hard stuff.*

Adam is always asking me if I'm a witch. He knows the answer. In this moment, I know it, too. I remember I can do magic. I close my eyes. In my mind, I surround my brother with sparkling white light. I imagine him healing and decide that's how it's going to go.

Johnny needed more time to heal, but ultimately, my magic worked. He was out of the hospital in a few weeks.

I really do have powers. So do you.

Just because an experience feels familiar doesn't mean it will go the way it did in the past. Energy reacts to rules. So when you assume similar experiences will go the same way again and again, the energy becomes hardwired to go that way. The same energetic frequency keeps repeating and stays on repeat until you consciously change it.

If, for example, you keep dating emotionally unavailable people—different versions of the same type—the pattern will continue until you interrupt it. To interrupt it, you have to start a new pattern, like dating emotionally *available* people.

Wayne Dyer said, "When you change the way you look at things, the things you look at change." That's the truth. You might not be able to change your past, but you can change how you see it. And you definitely have the power to create your future.

If something isn't working, tell yourself, God and the universe that you don't like it and that you're going to rewrite it. When you change your patterns, you change your life. You start to consider there could be another way, another possibility, an alternate existence where you have the health, wealth, love, relationships, career and life experiences you desire.

Rewriting is a form of rewiring. When we write, we get to say how things go. I now *know* that everything I desire exists for me as long as it's in alignment with my Greatest Level of Want. The funny thing about "desiring" and "deserving" is that there are only two letters of difference between them.

My initial desire was for Bo to stay here, but that was really a lower-level want. My *Greatest* Level of Want was for my brother to have peace and fulfill his life purpose. As a result, he got promoted to an angel. That's an important job, and as hard as I fought for him to stay here, I wouldn't want to stand in the way of the fulfillment of his ultimate mission. I see how many lives he's saved through our family's foundation and the scholarships created in his name. Bo's legacy lives on. One could argue he's able to make an even bigger impact from his office on the other side.

Of course, I wanted Grandad to live forever, too, but my Greatest Level of Want is to live out his legacy and teach others everything he taught me about business, generosity, family and life.

Growing up, my brothers were protective and loving. That was familiar to me. Lines got crossed later on when protective became controlling and love became obsession. From my daddy's girl upbringing to toxic relationships starting in my early teens, I've come a long way to understanding what love is and what it isn't.

I now know what trauma bonding is. I have a deep understanding of the young me who connected with the darkness in Kyle as I experienced an existential crisis of my own. I have compassion for the me of my late 20s who got engaged to Jesse during an intense battle with Lyme and the deep pain of losing my brother. I have so much love for the almost 30-year-old me who wanted a chance to redo everything that had come undone with PJ all those years earlier.

All I ever wanted was for love to come back to me.

My Greatest Level of Want is *love*. Period.

As you're manifesting and envisioning your desires, don't forget to check in and make sure that what looks good on your vision board is going to *feel* good too. Don't stubbornly keep fighting for a version of your reality that's not worthy of you like I did, time and time again. I tried to outsource my self-love anywhere I could, but in the end, it had to come back to me.

Eventually, I outgrew relationships that were no longer an energetic match—and not just in a spiritual "I'm out of your league" sort of way. I truly shifted, because I kept activating my own power, expanding my energy and learning how to glow in the dark.

The fear of loss is just the lack of belief that something greater exists. Something greater always exists when you believe in miracles.

You get to evolve. You get to become the next version of yourself, and, if you fully say yes to the spiritual journey, the person you are becoming will always feel better than the one you used to be.

Here's another prayer I wrote as I was learning to glow:

Always Be Evolving

As you rise, here's what will fall away...
People who are no longer a match,
Surroundings that are no longer a match,
Conversations that are no longer a match,
Excuses that are no longer a match.
Growth is not comfortable.
It will stretch you.
Challenge you.
Expand you.
Sometimes we need a soul shake-up
To reach our next level of evolution.
Don't be afraid.
Things fall apart so better things can fall together.
And in letting go of what doesn't fit,
We can receive what actually does.

PART FIVE
BYE

THIRTY-TWO
WILLING TO WALK AWAY

"You are a child of the universe no less than the trees and the stars; you have a right to be here. And whether or not it is clear to you, no doubt the universe is unfolding as it should."

—Max Ehrmann

I've asked myself a lot of questions in the process of making sense of the challenges life has brought me, but I've also never stopped trusting in the existence of something bigger than all of us. I can't help but think I must have some wild purpose if God let me go through all this madness and come out on the other side.

Like Beyoncé, I always believed in lemonade, making something sweet out of something sour. But nothing changed until the day I decided I really believed in *miracles*. A combination of faith and frustration got me down on my knees in full surrender. I knew I was at my rock bottom simply because I wasn't willing to get any lower. Looking back, I think I chose my rock bottom more than it chose me.

At my rock bottom, I got honest with God. I knew I had to break out of the old cycle of asking God to simply *bring* the things I wanted into my life. Instead, I asked for guidance to get there on my own. I asked for help in overcoming, in *rising*. It was a different kind of prayer—a mix of desperation, humility and responsibility—and I hoped it would bring a different kind of result.

I began to understand that as long as I was harboring resentment toward God and the great powers of the universe, I wouldn't be able to open myself to love again. Slowly but surely, by talking with God (which, to be honest, sometimes looked like writing in my journal, yelling in the car or crying during dance class), I learned to rebuild my internal system of faith and belief.

Through my struggles with disease, death and relationships, I asked God to guide me. Night after night, I said the prayers and wrote the affirmations you've read in this book. I don't know if I'd still be here without my faith in something greater than myself, so I was glad I already knew how to talk to God when the shit hit the fan. As my lists of worries were resolved one by one by divine forces—including myself—I went back to my journal and checked them off. As the list got shorter, I knew God, the universe and my future self were all listening.

As I allowed myself to feel vulnerable, start over and attract new experiences, I started to see the powers of the universe showing up for me. I learned about love, trust and belief and how they connect with the overall pursuit of happiness.

Regardless of your background, your upbringing or your faith, I think there's room for spiritual support and divine connection in your life. I don't believe in putting yourself in a box when it comes to big questions of faith. Whether you call it prayer, meditation or a really great pep talk, all you're doing when you connect to a higher power is *asking*, and in the end, it serves the same purpose that manifesting does: desiring and deciding. Just like me, you get to do spirituality on your own terms. It doesn't matter what anyone says, do it your way. You shouldn't have to keep your approach to faith a secret, but even if you do, let it be the secret that sets you free.

I invested a lot of time, money, energy and love during the years I was learning how to glow through what I was going through. I also let go of a lot of fear, limiting beliefs and playing small. I had to let go of some relationships, too. As you know, that's not my strong suit. I'm a lover and a fighter. I want things to *work*.

But life has taught me when to walk away from what doesn't feel right and how to tell when something is hurting more than it's helping. I still make big investments with my time, money, energy and love. I bring my all to the table of life. But no matter how much I've invested in the past, I'm willing to let go and that's an important development. I've become a woman who's willing to walk away.

The most significant part of a woman who's willing to walk away isn't what she's willing to walk away *from*. It's her trust and faith in what she's walking toward. It's in her belief that life, business, health, wealth and relationships can always get better no matter how they look at this exact moment. We're usually only willing to walk away when we know something greater exists *beyond* the letting go—when we know that holding on is what's keeping us stuck. Know that walking away is the decision that will open the doors to a better future. By clearing space, you open yourself to what's next.

My mom had a shopping rule when I was growing up. Before I hung up new purchases in my closet, I first had to give away any pieces I didn't want or need anymore. Sometimes, the giving away felt premature. I was afraid I might regret what I let go of, that I would want it back. But guess what. That never happened. Instead, I'd remember pieces I'd loved, search through my closet for them and then suddenly recall that I had given them away. I never had any regrets. I could always make sense of why I let those pieces go—the weird fit, the color that wasn't as flattering with my new highlights or the style I had grown out of. It works the same way when you walk away from relationships, situations and beliefs that no longer serve you.

When you empty your cup, life will refill it. And you have the power to believe, know and remember that the contents of your cup are always getting better. The shift doesn't always happen right away, which is why we can struggle to believe it's coming. But with trust and belief, we can stay open to love and possibility.

We are growing ourselves up and remembering who we were meant to be.

THIRTY-THREE

THE MOST IMPORTANT QUESTION

"Don't postpone joy."
—Edie Windsor

There's a tarot card I pull almost every time I do a reading. It's the Four of Cups, sometimes represented as the Four of Water. The Four of Cups tells me that the thing I *think* is the problem is actually the opportunity. Every time I see it, it's both annoying and expansive. Just imagine sitting cross-legged on your bed, asking for divine guidance. Again and again, the cards tell the same truth: *You're missing an opportunity.* See? Frustrating *and* expansive.

For years, with nearly every question I've asked and every struggle I've wrestled through, the cards have told me that it wasn't life that was malfunctioning. It was *me* missing an opportunity. Again and again, in regard to all sorts of questions and life challenges, the cards urged me to reevaluate my situation because the answer was right in front of me. All I needed to do was open my eyes to the possibilities.

For so long, I had been focusing on what I didn't have and taking for granted everything I did. I had bought into the belief that life was hard and it would always be that way. I felt victimized by my past, out of control in my current reality and hopeless about the future. It was a shitty way to live. Worst of all, it wasn't a phase. It was how I was living my entire life. Even my tarot cards knew it.

I haven't always been able to turn my biggest problems into my greatest opportunities. Even now, I have to work at it every day. Psychologists call it post-traumatic growth, but I call it glowing through what you're going through.

The most important question you will ever ask yourself is: *How is this an opportunity?*

There's an opportunity in every situation, but it's not always obvious. You might have to work to create it. But you can't let the bad shit that happens to you take you out of the game. Life's challenges *can* hold you back, but they don't *have* to. Bad experiences, painful memories and missed opportunities can discourage you because you're a human, at least in this lifetime. But you get a choice. You have a say. You get to decide. You can take the bad things and let them drag you down or you can use them as fuel to become the glow in the dark. I believe you have to glow after whatever you want.

Your purpose is actually quite simple. Your job in this lifetime is to create the thing you wish existed when you were stuck in the dark. Often, life will ask you to start creating it while you're still stuck. Do it anyway. You don't have to be healed to be happy.

You are not meant to suffer. Pain is a hard thing, but it doesn't have to *just* be a hard thing. Resilience is about coming back better, stronger and greater because of what you've been through.

How do you find the glow in the dark? You can start by seeing things as perfect even when they don't fit the definition of the perfect you *thought* you knew. This requires a radical shift in perspective.

There's a gift to discover in every loss and every disappointment. The key is choosing to see it that way. Loss, death and trauma don't naturally come with opportunity, and certainly not in an obvious way. But you can recreate them if you want to. Whenever something that initially feels disappointing happens, ask yourself and the universe to find the opportunity. You will get an answer, but don't rush the process. There's work to do along the way.

As you're learning to glow through what you go through, you have to evolve to meet your future self. You have to become the person who has what you say you want. You have to see yourself as worthy and capable of having everything you desire.

I've told you about my manifesting process and the steps most of us unknowingly skip. As we're seeing, feeling, being, doing and having our way to what we want, most of us forget the three middle pieces. Our instinct is to jump from seeing to having. We forget to start *feeling* the emotions of having what we want. We forget to start *being* the person who has what we want. As a result, we can't possibly start *doing* the things our future selves would do.

This is, in part, why we don't get what we say we want.

I want you to see how easy it is to manifest, so let's practice. Think of something you desire, big or small. Now, close your eyes and imagine the feeling of having it. Then imagine yourself as the future version of yourself who certainly has what you desire because it *is* certain. How is she *being?* What qualities do you notice? What is she *doing?* Seeing, feeling, being and doing will lead you to *having.*

During periods of doubt and questioning, go back to basics. Ask yourself: *What do I know to be true?* When you're in a hard place and can't yet see your way out, remember that God is not going to drop you off there. Either what you're manifesting will come through or something better will.

Your new prayer? *This or something better.*

We are always gaining and we are always losing. If we aim to lose what doesn't serve us (and often what doesn't *deserve* us) and focus on gaining what's more in alignment, our lives will improve.

THIRTY-FOUR

FINDING YOUR GLOW

"When we are no longer able to change a situation,
we are challenged to change ourselves."
—Viktor Frankl

I wish I'd had a guidebook as I was learning to glow through what I was going through. I didn't, but being alone on that path inspired me to create this one for you.

In my early years as a life and business coach, I started writing a course called Make Yourself Irresistible. The course was meant to be a deep dive into self-love and self-care. I was tired of the repetitive messaging that the key to attracting a lover was to focus on another person when I knew it was really about focusing on *yourself*. I wanted to show people that taking care of themselves—physically, mentally and emotionally—was the key to becoming irresistible. By shifting their focus, they would inevitably see their romantic dreams come to fruition.

I ended up turning the coursework into content for

Inner Glow Circle's curriculum, but I now realize that making yourself irresistible is the same as finding your G.L.O.W. or your Greatest Level of Want. When you glow, you're plugged into your highest-level desire for yourself and the world. From there, you become magnetic. It's inevitable.

It feels good to know what you want and go after it. It feels good to find your glow. And there's science to back that up! The experience of pleasure is driven by the release of neurotransmitters like dopamine in the brain. When you're in the constant practice of clarifying your desires and then consciously fulfilling them, you're stepping in to regulate your own dopamine levels. Since dopamine is associated with feelings of bliss, motivation and focus, going for what you want—and getting it—literally makes you glow. It's an internal reward system that's quite effective.

I used to think it had to be hard to be happy, but I don't see it that way anymore. Happiness is based on progress, perspective and possibility, and it doesn't have to be difficult to come by. It *does* take work to maintain. Bad things do happen. The trick is learning to rewrite those bad things, turn your pain into purpose and find the glow in the dark. You don't have to go looking for happiness because it's always looking for you. You just have to make yourself available.

One practice I use to get happy and stay there is called *Progress, Perspective and Possibility*.

Here's how this exercise came to me: One night I was feeling stressed and anxious. The weight of work was getting to me, and I was feeling overwhelmed with personal commitments. I wasn't seeing my progress; I had lost perspective and I certainly wasn't present to possibility. I got an idea.

I pulled out my calendar. I saw that 30 days earlier, I had just met with my editor and found out I had to rewrite an entire section of my book. I was feeling nervous and uncertain about my new relationship. I realized how far I had come in 30 days, rewriting all those pages and feeling happy and content with my new love. Now, I want to share this exercise with you.

Progress, Perspective and Possibility

PROGRESS IS SHORT TERM. To review your progress, first, scan back through your calendar.

What were you doing 30 days ago?

What were you working on?

Who were you meeting with?

What were you doing socially?

How were you feeling at those times?

Now, go back 90 days and repeat these questions.

Perspective is based on the longer term, so I flipped even further back through my calendar. I looked back one year, three years and five years.

Exactly one year ago, PJ had just told me he wanted to take a break. The next day, I could barely get out of bed. I felt broken. That feeling lasted for weeks until we got back together again.

Our recent permanent breakup, just a few weeks prior, was much easier on my system. I had become much stronger and much more emotionally resilient.

Three years ago, I was a year out from my breakup with Jesse and starting to date again. I still had Lyme and I had just recently regained ownership of my company after nearly a year-long battle.

Five years ago, Inner Glow Circle didn't even exist! I was still working for our family business, coaching and running Whole Glow spray tanning. I had also just started dating Jesse and entered what would become the scariest relationship of my life.

All three of those checkpoints gave me valuable perspective. I could see how far I'd come.

What were you doing and feeling one year ago?

Now, go back three years and five years and ask yourself the same question.

Possibility is about getting beyond the present moment, so I asked myself what was possible in the *next* 30 days. I knew I could at least match what I had done in the last 30 days, and since growth has an exponential effect, I figured I could move forward even more. I could complete another huge project and feel more confident in my relationships at home and at work.

I asked myself what was possible in the next year. I wrote down a date one year in the future. I wrote how old I would be. I wrote what was possible for my new book, new digital courses we were launching, new work partnerships and my new relationship. I also wrote how I wanted to feel —happier, more empowered, more at ease, loved, rejuvenated, more balanced and more in control of my life.

What's possible for you over the next 30 days?

What about the next year?

JUST KNOWING that unlimited possibilities exist for happiness—and that happiness is always looking for you—

shifts your energy. When you start believing it's possible to be really happy, you will feel more positive. As you feel more positive, you will attract more positive experiences. This alone will make you happier. You will see that your work is working. From there, life changes in response to you. You feel differently. You see things differently. You speak differently. You vibrate differently.

What are your limiting beliefs around happiness? Is there any part of you that thinks you aren't worthy of happiness? What part of you thinks you don't deserve it?

For me, sadness, stress and disappointment still come up daily. My reaction is different now because I know my feelings are real, but they are just feelings. I can honor them and then set them aside. I know how to move on. I can simply focus on my Greatest Level of Want—to be happy. This is the possibility I choose to live in.

You get to choose the possibility *you* live in, too.

Another one of my favorite practices can help you find your Greatest Level of Want on a daily basis. Do it every day, many times a day or as often as you need. Write your answers on paper, on your computer, in your phone notes or speak them out loud.

Find Your G.L.O.W. Daily Practice

AT THIS VERY MOMENT, if you could have anything you want without anyone questioning you, denying you or making fun of you for wanting it:

What would you want?
What would you want to see in your life?
How would you want to feel?

Who would you want to be?

What would you want to do?

What would you want to have?

What's not going the way you want lately?

What ideal solution(s) would make things the way you want them?

TAKING care of yourself and getting clear on your energy, your needs and your desires is the key to becoming irresistible. When you're operating with intention, you exude an open and expansive energy. That energy is what invites others in—to work with you, to collaborate with you, to fall in love with you.

Your mission as a human being is to become your youest you. If you stay open, everything around you will conspire to help bring forth the most potent version of you. You get to choose what you do with your life experiences, including your wins and your challenges. I suggest you let them teach you and inspire a level of happiness beyond what you've ever imagined. You deserve it.

THIRTY-FIVE

UNEXPECTED GRATITUDE

"Take the first step in faith. You don't have to see the whole staircase. Just take the first step."
—Martin Luther King Jr.

The self-help world says gratitude is everything, and when things feel shitty, gratitude can absolutely be an effective way to shift your mindset and refocus on what *is* working. But when things *really* suck, it can be hard to access any gratitude at all. It may seem fake, forced and entirely out of reach.

If you've weathered a major loss, survived trauma, struggled with your mental health or been faced with any of life's great challenges, you might have a funky relationship with gratitude, too.

Everything is connected, so if one area of your life has been uprooted, it can make your entire existence feel like a disaster. I get it. Though a common experience, this is where the vicious cycle begins: Grief keeps you from finding gratitude and the lack of gratitude for what *is* good creates more grief.

How do you get back to gratitude after grief? How do you discover the love within loss?

Enter *Unexpected Gratitude*, a practical strategy for making it through life's tough times.

I came up with this strategy because it was the thing *I* needed. One day, in the midst of all my losses, my mom told me to write a gratitude list. I was pissed. My brother was gone. I was sick. I wasn't grateful. But I challenged myself to dig deeper. I realized I could create gratitude from an unexpected place.

Unexpected Gratitude

1. *Write a list of everything you're not grateful for in this moment.* What are you frustrated with? What's annoying you? What feels overwhelming? What's making you sad or mad? What do you wish wasn't happening? What do you wish was different?

2. *Next, write down everything you have lost, are losing or fear you will lose.* Have you lost someone you love? Have you lost a job or an opportunity? Are your dreams being challenged? Is your reputation at risk? Are you losing touch with your purpose? Are you afraid of losing time, money or love?

3. *Now, write down everything you want to let go of but can't seem to.* Are you still hanging on to your ex? Are you beating yourself up over money you spent last month? Are

you hung up on that big mistake that happened at work?
Are you attached to how you thought your life was going to
look by now?

4. *Here's the big moment when you turn these challenges
into gratitude and find the glow in the dark.* Go through
everything you've written and ask yourself what you can be
grateful for. In the midst of all the challenges, where have
you experienced love? In the midst of all the sadness and
disappointment, where have you witnessed a miracle?
What miracles or opportunities are possible for the future?

FOR YEARS, my list of things I'd lost was long. I'd lost my
brother. I'd lost my health. I'd lost friends, dreams and
opportunities. I'd lost the person I'd known myself to be. I
wanted to let go of the pain, but I couldn't seem to hack it.
Eventually, though, I dug for the gratitude and found it. I
was grateful that my family telling the truth about Bo had
saved other lives. I was grateful I could empathize with
others who had chronic illness and tailor my work to serve
those people. The relationship was the hardest challenge to
find gratitude for, but in the end, the experience made me
fierce. It transformed me. I locked into my purpose more
deeply than ever before. And I was grateful for that.

When I looked hard enough and decided I would find
gratitude within myself, I *did*. If you want to survive and
thrive, you have to be willing to find the glow in the dark for
every situation in your life.

You can't outsource your grief, but I don't recommend
you do it alone, either. When you're in the dark, it's important to have access to two kinds of people: those who are

also in the dark, so you know you aren't alone and those who have found their way into the light, so you remember what's possible.

I hope you have a few people you can talk to as you practice finding the glow in the dark—and I mean *really* talk to. I hope you have people who will check in on you as you immerse yourself in the healing fires. If you *don't* already have those people around you, that's why therapists, coaches, acupuncturists, psychiatrists, astrologists, energy workers and healers of all kinds exist. I've utilized all of the above. Together, many of them helped save my life. Even if you have supportive family and friends, hiring help is still a game changer.

Hanging on to your anger and sadness isn't helping anyone. At times, I became righteous about my grief. It became part of my identity. Don't be like me. Honor the grief. Move through it. But know that it doesn't serve you to grip the rope as it rips through your hands, splintering your sweaty palms. Separate yourself from your losses and challenges. Don't let them become your identity.

Should is a lie, so I'm not going to say you "should" move on from wherever you are right now. But I do encourage you to ask yourself what you are holding on to. What are you waiting for? Are you waiting for a sign? Ask for it. Are you waiting for the right moment? Choose it. Are you waiting for the perfect opportunity? Create it.

Happiness and success are about finding your Greatest Level of Want and getting as close to it as you can. This will require you to take a lot of risks. I believe in failing, failing forward and failing on purpose.

After years of struggle, I got my own glow on. I would say I got my glow *back*, but the truth is, I got it on in a way I never had before. Almost overnight, my brown hair turned blonde. I replaced the dark blues in my home with beige and tan. Plants filled the rooms and brought new life to my space. I lightened things up on the outside and hoped the inside would follow suit.

Once you find your glow, the goal is to spend as much time as possible in your Glow Zone. Your Glow Zone is the area that lights you up the most. It's the work that's easiest, most natural and most fun. It brings you more joy than anything you've ever done before.

Being in the Glow Zone isn't in *getting* there—it's in *staying* there. It's like yoga. The key isn't getting into the pose—it's staying in it, relaxing and letting it benefit your body even if there is discomfort in the moment.

It doesn't matter where you are in your career, your relationships, your business, your finances or your health. We all get stuck and feel nervous, anxious or afraid. When you're stuck in fear, it's nearly impossible to see the light at the end of the tunnel or get clarity on the next step. Your desire to move forward will propel your healing.

Most of all, remember this: Whenever we're not getting what we desire, there's a part of us that's afraid of it. If you set a goal but still have resistance, doubts or limiting beliefs, the universe will pick up on it. Either you won't meet the goal at all or something will feel off when you do.

If you're falling short on a goal or a wish, ask yourself seriously if there's any part of you that doesn't want what you say you want. Is there any part of you that's resistant, doesn't feel good enough or feels unworthy of your goal? Do you have any confusion, fear, uncertainty, doubt or disbelief around your goal? If so, name it. Is there any part of your goal that doesn't align with your Greatest Level of Want?

If you uncover limiting beliefs about why you don't think you can have exactly what you want, take steps to work through them. Ask yourself: *Is there something bigger I desire beyond this momentary thing? If I'm honest with myself, do I have a Greater Level of Want, an even higher-level desire for myself, others and the world?*

When you get something different than what you said you wanted, ask yourself this: *What part of me actually wanted what I got? Where did I skip steps in the manifestation process? Who did I worry would get hurt or feel jealous if I reached my goal? What was I afraid people might say if I got what I wanted?*

You get to start fresh at any moment, and it's never too late to glow after what you want.

THIRTY-SIX

MAKING GOOD BY DOING GOOD

"I am lucky that whatever fear I have inside me, my desire to win is always stronger."
—Serena Williams

The ultimate happiness in life is finding your purpose and getting paid to live it. The getting paid part isn't as much about the money as it is the ability to make a living doing work you love, work that doesn't feel like "work."

It's validating. It's expansive. It's full of possibility. I've dedicated my life to finding my purpose and getting paid—and helping others do the same. It's become my North Star. That's why I created Inner Glow Circle.

I believe that if you can figure out how to live well, do good and give back to others while supporting your own wants and needs, you have found your purpose in life.

I hope you are leaving this experience with a renewed sense of grit, determination and focus, as well as strategies for finding the opportunity and becoming the glow in the dark every single day.

For me, the only thing that would make the pain I endured "worth it" would be saving other people from the years I spent searching for the meaning in loss.

There's nothing easy about learning how to glow through what you go through. But you may decide it's your only choice. I promise it's worth it. In the end, whatever you thought you lost will come back to you, too.

For a long time, looking good was the only part of life I felt I had any control over. Today, that's changed. I now know how to impact my thoughts, my actions and my reality. I know how to look good and feel good, and ultimately, I know those two things are inseparable for me.

You don't have to do what I've done or heal how I've healed. In fact, I encourage you to do it your own way. You know by now that the whole point is becoming your you-est you.

A final tip: As you go on your way and do the work to be happy, go easy on yourself. I'm a recovering perfectionist, too, but it's never going to be perfect. Chasing perfection is like being on a treadmill you can't turn off.

As you go through life and ask yourself, "Am I happy?" don't take your temperature on the hard days, the sick days or the generally cloudy days. The hard days will always lie. On those days, the thermometer is always broken.

Look for the clear days. Document them. Savor them. They're there and more are coming. Measure your happiness and your overall satisfaction with life on those days. Tell yourself that "I am happy" and then look for the evidence to support it.

Along the way, may you feel as good as you look and look as good as you feel. And remember, life gets to keep getting better and better. I'm going to leave you with one last prayer to take with you on your healing journey.

Today is complete.
There was love and letting go.
What has fallen away
Never belonged to me.
I am free.
I am grateful for this day.
It has made me better, stronger
And more grounded in my purpose.
Remove any burdens I am carrying.
Give me perspective,
Help me see my progress
And show me what's possible.
Remove my attachment to how things look,
Help me focus on how I feel and
Take away my obsession with perfection.
It is safe to let go.
It is safe to be free.
I ask for guidance in my sleep
And answers as I wake.

ACKNOWLEDGMENTS

Growing up, I felt so alone, and now I have so many people to thank. First, God, for the endless flow of miracles.

Mom, for telling me I can do anything; for the hours and hours of reading to me; for teaching me to have the highest attention to every detail. You knew I was special before I saw it at all.

Dad, for always encouraging a bigger vision; for teaching me that 99 percent of the things we worry about don't happen, but when they do, to face them head on. I will always look up to you.

Johnny, for surviving with me and for bringing our family new life. I know I can always count on you.

Thabata, for becoming the sister I always prayed for.

Johnny III, for being our miracle.

Gram, for teaching me beauty; Grandad, for your example; Mom-Mom, for your love of words; Pop-Pop, for breaking my heart open.

The Ritter, Cronin, Burns and DePaola families, for having our backs when we needed you most; Aunt Bobbie Lee, for showing up; Bridget, for leading the way; Aunt

Lynn, for bringing me to magic; Lesley, for *everything*; Aunt Sharon, for inspiring curiosity; Abbey, Lindsey, Kelsey, for being our sisters. Ashley and Jamie, for showing me the importance of family.

Liv, for becoming the greatest friend and partner, seven years and counting; for saying yes to my wild vision and then making it even wilder. I love sharing a brain with you.

Kelly, for your commitment, your brilliance and your friendship.

The entire Inner Glow Circle team—Lera, Hayley, Jaimie, Thea, Lentie, Nikki, Desi, Charisma, Roselle, Vee, Gigi, Sarah, our affiliates, students and graduates, now and in years to come—for changing lives that change other lives.

Lindsay, for nearly twenty years of friendship. You'll always be my Bandee.

Deven, for your loyalty and for making me laugh literally every time we speak.

Karen, for connecting me to the other side; for telling me I was meant to write books and when I asked what to write, saying, "Write what happened."

My teachers and friends: Ginny, for showing me the magic in the darkness; Nisha, for weaving beauty; Nadia, for teaching me to dance through pain; Jenn B.A., for your unwavering support; Theresa, for channeling messages; Dani, for your big, deep heart; Chelsey, for creating with me; Kim, for not letting me forget pleasure.

The team who worked so hard on this book and put up with my relentless perfectionism the whole way through: Alli H.K., for your patience and faith in me. You gave me the inspiration to face myself and tell these stories. Anna D., for bringing this to the finish line—and with it, bringing me to the finish line; Swan, for reminding me *why* every time I felt like giving up; Kaitlin, Ryan, Beth, Onur and everyone at Launch Pad publishing, for your confidence and reassurance.

Tina, Julie and Aisha, *at least I look good* on my book cover because of you!

Megan and Bridget H., for believing me.

Dr. V. and team, for all the laughs and all the healing. I literally wouldn't be here without you.

The PHP team at AAMC, for giving me a second chance at life.

Adam, for growing in friendship and love daily, taking on more so I could focus on bringing this dream to life and always reminding me to take my time. I love you.

Bo, for being *the real star* of all of this.

And you, my devoted reader and new friend, for your time, willingness and faith in me. We really can glow through whatever we go through.

TO MY READER

Thank you for trusting me with your heart and for taking the time to read *At Least You Look Good: Learning to Glow Through What You Go Through.* I hope you feel prepared to glow through whatever life brings your way. One of the best ways for emerging authors to gain exposure and get their books into the hands of the people who need them most is through book reviews. It would mean the world to me if you could take five minutes to write a review of *At Least You Look Good* on Amazon.

Don't forget to visit innerglowcircle.com/training and innerglowcircle.com/manifesting and download the two free workshops that I shared with you in this book. I am so grateful for you!

Connect with me on Instagram:
    @itskatiedepaola
    @innerglowcircle

ABOUT THE AUTHOR

Katie DePaola is an author, speaker, entrepreneur and the founder of Inner Glow Circle, a company dedicated to helping women entrepreneurs find their glow and live purpose-driven lives, which has grown into a globally recognized training program. She has been featured in TIME, Entrepreneur and Forbes. Katie lives in Washington, DC where she serves on the board for Bo's Effort and occasionally enjoys building her business from the bathtub.